Praise for *All the Waking Hours*

"Erin Wunker's *All the Waking Hours* drew me in immediately with its soothing voice and tone, bringing me back to the days of early motherhood. What a thoughtful inward and outward meditation on boredom and bother, but one that ultimately transforms into a meditation about time and mortality. These meditations invite the reader to travel along with a thoughtful and intelligent mind."

—Victoria Chang, author of *Obit* and *With My Back to the World*

"How do we know if the life we are living is really ours? And how do we show up for the people we love and care for? These are, above all, questions of attention. In stunning and incisive prose, Erin Wunker blends memoir and cultural criticism and philosophy to weave a profound portrait of what it means to notice. With a fierce wisdom, Wunker goes straight at the raw unanswered questions we too often ignore to get on with our days. This book is begging you not to get on with your day until you've mapped your innermost seas. Wunker writes with brio and rigour about not letting yourself off the hook, even in the most mundane moments, especially in the most mundane moments."

—Elamin Abdelmahmoud, author of *Son of Elsewhere*

"With her deep sense of history and agile intellect, Erin Wunker has made a book of many riches. Her narrations of early motherhood surprise and amuse in equal measure without compromising the fierce and poetic thinking that is everywhere present in *All the Waking Hours*. This book meets the challenge of what it means to mother in dark times, proving as expansive as the act of assembling decades of hard-won wisdom in the direction of subtly vivid prose, and in service of vital and ethical hopes."

—Canisia Lubrin, author of *Code Noir*

"A beautifully written, kaleidoscopic book that swirls through boredom's fertile childhood pleasures, caregiving's elations/tediums, and a late capitalist mediascape that encourages us to swallow the world, and its suffering, with a yawn. With great sensory attunement and a meticulously observant mind, Erin Wunker has written a very un-boring collection, a gift for wild, anxious, inconsolable readers, and a study in how to meet one's private and public hours with greater curiosity, communion, and wakeful intention."

—Kyo Maclear, author of *Unearthing* and *Birds Art Life*

"All at once insightful, devastating, and beautiful, *All the Waking Hours* is an impressive feat of both observation and intellect. Wunker has thoughtfully created a space to explore some of the more difficult aspects of being a mother, of being a woman, of being alive, and we feel safe in her care. We are all so lucky to have Wunker's incredible voice, mind, and heart, and her uncanny ability to make connections—a true gem of a collection."

—Stacey May Fowles, author of *Baseball Life Advice* and *The Lost Season*

ALL THE WAKING HOURS

ESSAYS

ERIN WUNKER

Assembly Press
Prince Edward County, Ontario

Library and Archives Canada Cataloguing in Publication
Title: All the waking hours : essays / Erin Wunker.
Names: Wunker, Erin, 1979- author.
Identifiers: Canadiana (print) 20260207136 | Canadiana (ebook) 20260207144 | ISBN 9781998336333 (softcover) | ISBN 9781998336340 (EPUB)
Subjects: LCSH: Wunker, Erin, 1979- | LCSH: Feminist theory. | LCSH: Feminism. | LCSH: Women—Psychology. | LCSH: Women—Conduct of life. | LCGFT: Essays. | LCGFT: Memoirs.
Classification: LCC HQ1190 .W84 2026 | DDC 305.4201—dc23

Published by Assembly Press | assemblypress.ca
Cover and interior design by Greg Tabor
Edited by Andrew Faulkner

Printed and bound in Canada on uncoated paper made from recycled content in line with our commitment to ethical business practices and sustainability.

Canada Council for the Arts | Conseil des Arts du Canada
ONTARIO ARTS COUNCIL
CONSEIL DES ARTS DE L'ONTARIO
an Ontario government agency
un organisme du gouvernement de l'Ontario

With the participation of the Government of Canada
Avec la participation du gouvernement du Canada | Canada

CONTENTS

ALL THE WAKING HOURS

ON THE PUBLIC RISKS OF BEING BORED AND BEING A WOMAN

"I'm a bit bored," I admitted, in hushed tones, to an acquaintance in the early months of new motherhood. I was quieted with a look of disapproval. Surely, I wasn't bored. Not with all this new life, this new responsibility. Right? I felt chastened.

Later, I overheard a whisper: "She must have postpartum depression." It was a judgement doled out by someone I hardly knew, and yet it hung like a lead weight on a fishing line. It felt like a slap; it felt like a diagnosis; it felt like a label affixed to my forehead. I carried this throwaway comment with me for too long. Maybe I was depressed or bothered, or maybe I was just bored. I was certainly disoriented. I was also caring and loving and attending. I was awestruck and I was also tired. Yes, my states and actions were in tension with one another. And so, with the focus of a predator, I circled those feelings to understand their habits and movements. But I worried that what I found would be pathologized by others. There was no room for being bored as a new mother. There was no room for other possibilities or curiosity or care. That passing comment lodged itself, splinter-like, in my mind. I said and wrote many words about motherhood, but I did not say I was bored again.

* * *

A few years later, on a Monday morning, because of course it was a Monday, I again bumped up against the complexities of my interior life. The day was cold, clear, and sunny. The air was filled with frost and the fine dust that coats every surface when the light is just so. I had spent the weekend in a frenzy of energized cleaning, yet there were still cobwebs drifting from the ceiling to the wall, just out of reach, right in my sightline as my three-year-old and I ate breakfast in a weekday rush. Mornings, in this period, felt ungovernable regardless of when I woke. It occurred to me often that this feeling I had might, in fact, be conditioned by external forces—jobs, childcare, the navigation of life in late capitalism—but this insight soothed nothing in me. That particular morning, my partner was out of town for work. I had risen eye-wateringly early and attended to all the small and vital morning tasks. Hair had been brushed. Teeth too. We set out. All the bags, packed, were strapped to me. I could have driven to daycare, I suppose, but it didn't occur to me. I prefer to go under my own steam.

So we walked, me and my small child. In the cold, we walked. Through steam hiccupping from buildings, we walked. Across the windswept Halifax Commons, we walked, bitten by cold. Mittened hands raised themselves to my waist, and so I carried her, too. My arms ached. My hands were clenched beneath her in the kind of fireman's carry I'd learned in life-saving courses. No slipping, I thought to myself over and over. We made it to daycare and after she clamoured to open the door, she was back in my arms (still aching) and somehow we made it up the stairs. We were five minutes early, and I would in turn make my meeting on time.

But no. Her small stuffed unicorn—beloved, ragged with love—had fallen. Where? Where? Back down the stairs. Out the door in a mix of panic and fury. Up the hill. Past the needle exchange, past the new doughnut shop, past the plastic-free bulk store. No stuffie. Across the Commons. Nothing. All the while picturing that little face. All the while feeling rage (why rage?) and shame (always shame). Why didn't she hold on more tightly? Why did I think I could carry everything? When did they become "stuffies" anyhow? I can conjure the smell of my own stuffed animals still. The way I'd pushed my face into them to quiet my own crying. Their placid brown-black eyes always ready for hugs or tears or adventure. Where did they go? Lost in moves between countries. Abandoned in parking-lot donation bins. Packed in plastic when I came home with lice, and my mother, white-lipped with frustration, combed through my hair while I sat on the steps beside the bee-filled forsythia.

British pediatrician and psychoanalyst D. W. Winnicott has a theory about child development and transitional objects: they are sovereign to the child herself and vital to her development. They must never change, he writes, unless directed by the child.

Unbelievably, I found my daughter's stuffie. I found the unicorn. There, under the doorbell of the daycare to which

I had returned, defeated. The same door I had spilled out of a quarter of an hour before, too panicked and frustrated to spot the white and pink fur against the asphalt. There, dropped from a little mittened hand. That gorgeous mittened hand. I grabbed the unicorn. Burst back into the daycare, triumphant, still annoyed. Interrupted the people on break who care for our child all day to tell them of my triumph. And as I was in the midst of telling them, I was struck by the predictability of my story and the indulgence of my need to tell it in the breakroom quiet that I had shattered. With this realization of the banality of my spirited declarations after my own self-induced frenzy, I was ashamed and immediately bored with myself and by my big, strange feelings. I left. Late for everything. It was not quite nine a.m.

* * *

Boredom is an ideology. It is an oppositional relationship that has emerged in free-market capitalism. There is nothing free about time that is unfettered. It is easier for me to recognize this when I encounter other people's boredom, which happens most often when I read. There, boredom is tied to work, to the demands the world and situations place on the characters. From this vista, I recognize that boredom is so often yoked to gender. Boredom is sutured to class. Boredom is uneven in its distribution, and it has many guises. Boredom is my partner's mother, exhausted after a twelve-hour Emerg shift in a small-town hospital but wide awake in front of the television. Boredom is a temporary foreign worker, after finishing a shift cleaning rooms at a motel in rural Manitoba, trying to reach loved ones in another time zone. Boredom is two hours off between a swing shift. Boredom is "free time" that is not free. Boredom is the reaching that the mind must do. Boredom is a mind held taut by internalized imperatives to do and keep doing.

Sometimes, it is true that boredom has a chimeric relationship with depression. The restlessness that has led to me stalking these feelings was born with both names—boredom, depression—as potential signposts. For Ann Cvetkovich, who writes about gender and public feelings at the University of Texas at Austin, the term *depression* is as telling as the term *boredom*. Like a canary in the coal mine, caged for the sole purpose of signalling danger to others, depression indicates something big in the atmosphere of the self. Like boredom, depression references everything and nothing, so Cvetkovich, a scholar, reaches across time for another word, another concept. What she finds in the archives is acedia. Originating from the Greeks, acedia in this sense belongs to early Christian monks, whose daily work was self-scrutiny and reflection. Their ultimate aim was to get closer to God. Sometimes, though, their self-scrutiny would consume them. In these cases, rather than inching closer to divinity, a monk would experience what the fourth-century writer John Cassian called "a weariness of the heart." A distressed heart. A stalled engine. A heart sinking below the water's surface. The primary symptom of acedia was a forgetfulness of one's purpose. Acedia was spiritual despair. A sin, in other words. But for Cvetkovich, acedia is a useful point on a map of being a person in the present.

Acedia offers a place to think about the pervasiveness of bad feelings that are difficult to attach to preceding events. Cvetkovich aligns the restless boredom of the sad soul with contemporary conditions. Sadness without a clear inciting cause, boredom even though there are so many things to do—these are symptoms of a larger political depression that is a conceptual bridge between emotional and political life. In other words, there are a host of reasons to feel bad and also bored. So many, in fact, that they become a body of water in which we swim. Perhaps, then, my bad feelings, my boredoms, are not simply markers of postpartum pathologies. Perhaps these bad feelings are pinpricks of light looking to constellate connections I was only just starting to name. Not just *woman*, but *mother*, for example. Not only weary in my heart, but also weary with the public narratives mapped onto any names for any of the feelings I speak aloud.

⋆ ⋆ ⋆

Time passed. I built myself into a person who filled each minute with action and called it meaningful, called myself useful. This is learned and polished behaviour, and it makes me efficient in my own way. I can cross tasks off a list with the speed of a tiger shark. I have managed and multi-tasked, taken on more than my share as a precarious worker, carried all the groceries in at once to "save time." I have said "I can take care of it on my own" when offered help simply to appear capable, especially to myself. I have accomplished in a state of repetitiveness that I called boredom. And when I became a mother, I felt that boredom shift tectonically. My body became soft under hours of nursing a newborn. I marvelled, but I also raged. Sharing my time—myself—with a small creature made me feel raw and tender and also tedious. While tending to another, time is expansive, endless, though the tenor of that endlessness chimes a different note than it does when I am solitary. So, yes, boredom gets mixed up with sadness sometimes. I acknowledged this in my midnight thoughts, which are much like the midnight zone, that place in the ocean I've learned about from a children's program. The light is different in the midnight zone. It is too deep for the surface light to reach; creatures in the midnight zone have to make their own light.

* * *

Perhaps *boring* isn't the most accurate word. A therapist tells me to be kinder to myself. In turn, I tell myself to stop being so self-absorbed. We both may be right, a bit, though that doesn't matter when a middle-of-the-night wail wakes me from a dream where I'm trying to get somewhere but I'm hopelessly late despite running. I still sometimes lie in the midnight zone and think midnight thoughts. Why does the dog breathe so loudly? Have I lost feeling in the left side of my body? Is it always this hot in here? What, really, did Simone Weil mean when she said we need roots, all of us? How is it possible to move through time and not become mean? Is this all durational performance art? Will I have time to buy milk after the gym and get home before the house wakes? Will I always feel this pull of sadness at the temporality of it all, the fleetingness? Is March not the cruelest month, rather than April? Will I ever stop tearing up at the thought of my child's gorgeous nose? Will I ever write again? What is the internet but another box that, when opened by a deeply curious femme, attacks her in her wild desire for knowledge? Did

I pay the phone bill? Can I? And then: when did I last see this hour of morning?

I am not a wakeful person. I am a person who is dutifully awake. I feel as if, should I rise early enough, I can beat the noonday demon away from the door of my heart. If I am organized enough, prepared enough. If I can exhaust my body with exercise before dawn, then surely I will be able to be kind. I wake to the alarm on my phone, which I have placed under two pillows to keep from disturbing anyone else in the house. Of course, the dog wakes anyway. I used to wake to a pulse that rabbited in my chest. I used to wake with rage and despair in my mouth. Now I wake to answer a call that has been set by a previous, more ambitious version of myself. Down the stairs for coffee with milk. Out the door into the darkness of night's shoulder. All this stalking of feelings, all this vigilance, all this self-reflection is for something. I know that now. If, as poet Sue Goyette writes in a long poem about human failures, a bear can nudge at the word *mother* and sometimes find it lacking, then I can too.

It takes a massive amount of energy for a creature who lives in the midnight zone to make light. The effort is staggering to comprehend. The effort tires me, and still I work to generate light as a secular blessing, my own earnest Care Bear Stare or modest spell for the world. Who knows why any person thinks what they think unless they bless you with their story? In the kitchen, cold, dark, a blessing to be awake so early with the dog beside me. One blessing among many. I think this as I pad my bare feet across the floor, feeling the grit of the sidewalk that has worked its way indoors.

What company, the dog, who, steadfast in his witness, thinks only of a walk. Of a run. What blessings are these little pinpoints of light that are working me toward something bigger than the things I name *boredom*.

Bless the espresso machine. Bless breakfast, laid out and waiting. Bless a clean counter and a stack of done dishes in the drying rack. Bless the folded clothes and the clean bathroom. Bless a hug, given from behind and with love. Bless the idea of a mitten box by the door. Bless reading. Bless the patience and desire I now have for the things that once made me paw the ground with impatience, like the dog, thinking of a run. Bless the care and kindness of a friend. Bless the weekly potlucks that pull us through the winter. Bless salt. Bless Lot's wife, never named, but bless her for looking back, wistful and wondering. Bless my beloved. Bless this child in the room above who, with luck, will inherit more than my pathos.

ON WISDOM AND THE WEATHER

Say the girl or animal again wakes up.
Lisa Robertson

When I was small—five or six—I spent one summer three different ways. There were long days in my great-aunt's care, there were long days in my maternal grandmother's care, and there were stretches when I was truly alone. To be truly alone at that time was a rare and delicious freedom. To be cared for was a gift, I know now, but one that was entwined with boredom and other bothers. My parents had a business and were inundated with tasks from dawn to well past dusk. I know this in hindsight, but in truth, when I touch that time in my memory, all I get is a hazy lack of clarity around their images. Where were they really? All of this period is shot through with contradictions. I can't recall, for example, if my paternal great-aunt and my maternal grandmother knew one another. It is unlikely that they wouldn't have, but I do come from people who silo, as in, those are church friends, and these are school friends. As in, this is my grandmother Ruth, from the farm in Pennsylvania, and that is my great-aunt Bess from Toronto. As in, mind your business and I'll do the same.

Don't ask me what was going on in my house in those years. I couldn't tell you. Too young, too involved in figuring out how to be a good child. Too solitary. Too nose in a book. Too head in the trees. Incidentally, the trees have changed since those years. Some have come down in hard winds.

Older memories hold different atmospheres at their edges. These memories are muggy and close, like the air before rain. They are unlike the atmospheres I move through now, but I only realize this when I try to recall what it felt like to be small. The atmospheres I am moving through in these, my middle years, are clearer, mostly. There's a memory game I play to try to understand why my childhood memories are so foggy. In my mind's eye, I try to picture a room or an object from that time as clearly as possible. Usually, it comes into view like a photograph in developer. Once I can see that space or thing clearly, I touch it with my mind and wait to feel something. An electric shock, or the hairs on the back of my neck standing up. Maybe a sense of calm. The feeling is information; the image is the catalyst. My job is to figure out what each means, and what's worth holding on to. Maybe I do this when I need to remind myself that I am, in fact, wiser than I have been. Maybe I do it to remember I have always had an animal instinct. What is certain is that the questions I ask myself matter, especially when those questions are trying to probe the origin of a storm.

Bess, my great-aunt, lived alone for fifty years in a two-storey bay-and-gable brick house a few blocks from the house where she'd grown up. I loved her house. It had such an otherworldly light, and black-and-white bathroom tiles, which struck me as the height of luxury. Her house was full to the rafters with books. Books were on shelves; they were also in piles on the floor beside the couch, and in stacks around the unused piano. The house had been new when Bess moved into it with her husband sometime in the 1940s. By the time I rolled around, it no longer looked new, but neither did it look in disarray. It looked the way I imagine a messy mind might look: everything curious and peculiar and filled with potential, but lord, overwhelming would be an understatement.

Bess, I was told, had married late. What does it mean to marry late? What is marrying on time? No one had that answer for me. Her husband died five years into their marriage, and Bess remained single ever after. By all accounts, Bess's husband, Walter, was a dapper man with a decent amount of spending money. Many of the piled-up books I navigated in her house were actually his. Walter's books were leather-bound editions, mainly from the Everyman's Library Classics series. Long after Bess died, my father built a room for these books that had been Walter's, then Bess's.

I wonder, sometimes, how I would have turned out if Walter's reading tastes had been different. I read Thomas Hardy, George Eliot, and Charles Dickens, and developed a taste for the bleak. I wonder, now, who I might have been if, instead of spending time with the ill-fated Maggie Tulliver of *The Mill on the Floss,* I'd read George Sand writing her own restless perseverance (all while wearing her lover Chopin's pants). Instead, I spent my time with *Jude the Obscure*, considering alienation and failed attempts at the farming life.

Bess's house was fascinating and frightening, a little like Bess herself. Both house and Bess seemed like too much and also not enough. Too many things, too many accessories, too many books crowding the porcelain knick-knacks from Germany and England. Yet, both house and Bess had a kind of enticing other-worldliness to them, as if they had been ferried across a stormy sea in a suitcase and spent all the time since wondering how they ended up here, and why.

Bess's house was in a central part of a big city, but I don't recall spending time outside more than once or twice. There was no yard to speak of, only a small sliver of weedy alleyway with the potential surprise of nearby neighbours, though I can't remember meeting any. Where were all the people, I wondered. At home, we had a square backyard hemmed in by purple lilacs. I had a little playhouse that my father and great-uncle built one tense weekend. We also had a fish pond, which I avoided after tumbling into it once, to the ringing laughter of our next-door neighbour. I found him fascinating, that neighbour, with his Tom Selleck moustache and his cigars, and I'd made a little wooden sculpture for him, which I was on my way to pass through the hedge when I fell. I was so excited to get there, so proud of my work, that I forgot the sunken pond. It was small, but I still fell into water over my head. The water was murky, and filled with leaves and worms. I was terrified before I was mortified. My father fished me out by my hood. I was still clutching my work, so I passed it to the neighbour, who was doubled over laughing. Joe was his name. As I sloshed away, I saw Joe toss my work onto his woodpile. Going forward, I conceived of neighbours as an ever-present, double-edged source of both joy and mockery, which meant that the absence of other people at Bess's gave it a feeling of being unmoored from the rest of the world. Like only her and I existed, at least while I was there.

Days with Bess were long. She had no television, and while I was allowed to read, I tended to wake early. That stretched the day out in all directions. I stayed inside and wandered slowly through the house, making a mental inventory of oddities. There was the mantel covered in little porcelain and glass figures, and greeting cards from every conceivable holiday, but my favourite spot to park myself was in front of one glass-doored cabinet. Like the mantel, it too was filled with tiny figurines. There was a small, pointed shoe that was also an ashtray (unused). Beside it was a glass sphere with red, blue, and yellow glass flowers trapped within it. Another shelf held a porcelain basket painted pink and blue with twisting vines of flowers running along its sides and up the handle. Nearby, a blue lion, also breakable. A lacquered box. A pair of unused leather gloves that looked deflated, despite each of the dozen tiny buttons along the sides being done up tight. I was not allowed to touch any of these objects, which fed my nearly irresistible wish to put my hands on them. Each room held more things than seemed possible. Stacks of paper dotted every surface, and sometimes single pages would float to the floor when I walked by.

On the windowsill in the dining room, amidst the books and cabinets, sat a single struggling African violet. My great-aunt was mad for African violets, but she couldn't seem to keep them alive. My mother, on the other hand, was going through a geranium phase that summer, and our house was punctuated with their earthy fug. I liked to surreptitiously stroke the African violet's velvet leaves. This might have been why Bess's plant did not thrive. In the pot along with the violet was a postcard bearing an image of a woman in a long dress. The postcard had never been sent and looked like it had been sitting in moist soil forever. Watermarks had crept up the cardboard in craggy brown lines, and I had the sense that if I tugged it, the lower part of the card would rip right off.

I paid close attention to this card, which I thought of as the "Weather Dress." When it was cool, the skirt turned a deep purple, which made me wonder if it was there to coax the African violent into reluctant bloom. When it was hot, the Dress was a kind of muted grey. Once, I watered the violet and watched as the Dress decided what to do. It went blue green halfway up the lady's legs then stopped, as if she'd stepped into a knee-deep puddle.

The Weather Dress was a hygroscope. While plants and other organisms have known about it forever, humans only started experimenting and writing about hygroscopy in 1790. A hygroscope measures the humidity in the air, which seems important. What is humidity, really? Invisible to the human eye, humidity is the amount of water vapour present in the air. In other words, it is the unseen thing that makes a place feel more or less tolerable, or, at least, that's how it seems to me. I'd look at the postcard and imagine some wise girl out under the clouds, lifting her head to check the weather

Like the Weather Dress girl, Bess herself wore dresses that stopped just below the knee. All her dresses were of the same cut and fabric. They were short-sleeved sack affairs made of a slippery polyester, each one a dizzy pattern of paisley, large flowers, or peacock feathers. Over these, Bess wore one of her endless crocheted cardigans held together at the neck by a clip. She favoured ankle socks and wedge-heeled slingbacks in all seasons. Her glasses were cat eyes, her hair an iron-grey flapper bob. Her outfits were baffling to me, and her moods more so. One day she was the double-dutching auntie who set down her groceries and hopped over a skipping rope with ease. The next, Bess was the sharp disciplinarian who looked on my small rebellions with disdain. I learned swiftly that I was most palatable for her when I was curled up with a book. When does a child sniff the air and start to recognize the emotional weather? I was not a wise girl at first, but I learned quickly to become one.

If I wasn't with Bess, I was with my maternal grandmother. She had driven from America to help mind me while my parents worked to get their bearings. That's how she put it. I'm minding her. My mother's mother had a difficult upbringing, or, at least, that was the story. She was smart, but she'd endured what would today be diagnosed as a learning disability, likely more specifically as dyslexia. She had trouble with reading, and her spelling remained deeply creative until her death at age ninety-nine and a half. This difficulty meant she'd left school after seventh grade and gone to work as a house cleaner. She became a farmer's wife, until he died suddenly. These events and departures changed the landscape of her future.

What I try to imagine is how that felt in the moments after big changes happened. I imagine the moment before a tsunami hits, when a beach is first flooded and then the sea sucks the ocean back. Imagine the sound between the water's departure and its colossal return.

My grandmother could be fun, and she could also be a menace. This was true, especially around sleep. For long past the time I was nap-aged, my grandmother would enforce an afternoon rest. To ensure that daily stillness happened to my body, she would sit in the nap room and snap her fingers in my face if I shifted. If this restlessness happened more than a few times, she'd trade the snaps for something firmer. My cousin, who was from France and came to visit for a month each summer, would sometimes get roped into these mandatory naps. She was a shade younger than me, and yet she argued back at my grandmother's demands for rest, which I admired. My small, strong cousin would put her hands on her slim hips and yell at my grandmother in French, a language my grandmother did not comprehend. My grandmother, a monoglot, would yell back in English until they both tired. Then, she would take my cousin out of the room and make her toast. I listened to them play cards while I lay sweating in the nap room.

There was no double-dutching out of the way of my grandmother's moods the way there was with Bess. My grandmother took me reading a book as a light taunting. Her moods were like storms, often upon you before you knew it. I learned, instead, to keep my rain boots handy, so to speak. Eventually, I would be old enough to wash dishes in the kitchen of my parents' family business. Until then, I would have to find other ways to ride out the weather.

* * *

Let me try to play it straight. What I really mean is that there is wisdom beyond language that some of us have to learn, and learn early. Like knowing when to come out of the water when lightening moves closer, or like spotting clouds shifting from moody to murderous and knowing when to take cover. Learning to read the weather and its shifts is a good skill. It has kept me safe in certain circumstances and allowed me to be bombastic in others. I hope it has helped shape me into an attentive listener. I am beginning to suspect, though, that becoming skilled at reading the complex weather of others has kept me from learning how to recognize my own. This might also have been true for the women I learned from as well, but I didn't have the kind of relationship with them to talk things out. I was too young. They were my elders. And anyway, I know for sure I wouldn't have thought to ask. Still, it occurs to me now that if navigating the storms of others are an organizing principle in my own life, I still have rather a lot to learn.

* * *

Bess married late and for love and then was widowed. She raised her sister, who was seventeen years younger. Bess was also a deaconess in the Anglican church. She was stern and sweet in wildly unpredictable ways that could frighten a child. She called me petekind, an unexpected diminutive, as her people were English and Irish, not Dutch. She talked a blue streak until a stroke took her voice, and then she spoke with her eyes. In other words, the facts I know of her are only the tent poles in the story of a life. When she died, frustrated and silent in the locked box of her broken body, I was not taken to the funeral. It was as though she had vanished into ether.

My grandmother had left her mother's house at thirteen. She married and then was widowed. The farm was sold. She drove circuits around the Northeast to mind the various grandchildren. When she died, softened and sweet in her tenth decade, the barometer in me shifted. Both these women shared one belief, and it is this: a good girl knows her place, and in that place, she'd best learn to tell the weather. This is a trick, I have come to think. Who gets to say what place is hers and what makes her good? Not the girl, of that I am certain.

* * *

Years after Bess died, I found myself living in a shack at the bottom of a western mountain. I had arrived at the mountain town with a small plan that slipped like water through my cupped hands. Planless, I went looking for any sign of what to do with my life, and that's how I found myself waiting to get my tea leaves read in a small kitchen in Cranbrook, British Columbia. The reader, who wore several patterns of gingham and a large wool cardigan, looked into my cup and told me what she saw. There was uncertainty, but also always housing. There were books and crevasses that felt too big to get out of, but there I was each time on the other side. And here—strange!— the reader paused and tilted the cup. There was a woman who was shaped like a mushroom sitting on a pile of books, and she was holding an umbrella and looking stern, and another woman looker sterner still. Did I know who these women were, the reader wondered. I did, indeed. The tea-leaf reader told me that these women were nudging me forward out of my sad rut. She also said their stubbornness and sternness was a lesson I'd already learned, and that it was time to learn new things. In less than a month I had packed my car, driven back across the country, and launched myself into life in a city whose first language was not my own. The first things I bought when I arrived were an umbrella and a book.

* * *

I realize now that I learned to wake up, as Lisa Robertson suggests girls do. I learned to wake up, and from my great-aunt and my grandmother I learned, however slant, to ready myself for any weather.

ON SWIMMING

I believe that always, or almost always, in all childhoods and in all the lives that follow them, the mother represents madness. Our mothers always remain the strangest, craziest people we've ever met.

Marguerite Duras

My childhood summers were spent beside a lake named for its shape. Gull Foot Lake was shortened in the mid-twentieth century to Gull Lake. Like the lake, the word *gull* has multiple personalities. Shorebird, yes, and also one who is easy to fool.

A fish brought my ancestors to this lake. My great-grandparents and their three sons had been travelling in a tent caravan in Depression-era America when, at a revival, they befriended a preacher from Canada. The preacher was a kind and personable man. My great-grandfather was not. A former rum-runner and headstrong patriarch, and an amiable travelling preacher who loved the outdoors—they bonded over a shared love of fishing, and, when they parted ways, planned to stay in touch. Years later, the preacher, by then known as one of the only people capable of getting my great-grandfather to listen to sense, sent a photo of himself to my great-grandfather. In the photo, the preacher was holding a bass at shoulder height. The fish's tail hung nearly to his knees. The preacher wrote that he'd caught the fish near a lodge that was for sale, located in a place a Canadian Royal Commission would later declare "a grave settlement mistake." A place where the colonial project of moving people to cultivate land failed, mainly due to settlers' failure to thrive. The land was so hard and the weather so harsh that suicide rates skyrocketed.

The photograph is framed and hangs on a wall beside the taxidermized fish. I imagine the fish from the photograph opening its mouth in early spring, moving more swiftly as the water slowly warms. I wonder what it thought when it gulped down the pastor's lure. My great-grandfather, hungry with hope for a new adventure, saw in that photo enough promise to pull up stakes and cross a border. Was he lured by magic or belief or madness? Whichever it was, my ancestors came to this granite-packed place south of Canoe Lake, where the famous painter Tom Thomson fell into the water—he had been fishing too—and didn't get out. My people took up residence in a dilapidated hunting and fishing lodge called Miners' Bay and ran it for eight decades. When it was my parents' turn in the early 1990s, the advertising pamphlets still read *NO ROWDYISM*. When I am asked what it was like to live there, I describe it as *Dirty Dancing* run by Baptists, and that is a bit true. God, the last hopes of a teetotalling retired rum-runner, and a big fish: that's how I came to know this lake, where we returned each summer.

In the middle of the lake, most of it just below the surface, is Gull Rock, a massive remnant of the lake's own becoming. The birds have claimed it as their own. Without their white and grey bodies sitting, sunning, and floating nearby, without the whitewash of bird shit on the small bit breaking the water's surface, the huge rock would be nearly impossible to spot. At age ten or so, I was allowed to take the motorboat out alone, and I remember steering as far as possible from the rock, as if it might throw itself in front of the hull should my attention waver.

A pipe ran from the lake right into my parents' cottage, which sits on the same bay as the lodge. While you weren't meant to drink the water, I always thought about drinking it, especially in the shower. Mouth open, face tilted up, I'd swish around a few warm mouthfuls. Then, scared, I'd spit them into the tub and watch them drain away. The pipe that brought the water to the cottage was darkened by weather and well camouflaged among rusty pine needles that layered the ground in a slippery shag carpet. Once, barefoot, I tripped over the pipe and tore the softest part of my big toe. The nail came off and grew back poorly. For the rest of that summer I sat for twenty minutes twice a day, foot in warm peroxide, coaxing the infection out under my mother's orders.

Just around the corner from the pipe, right next to the lake, was a small, shallow natural basin in the granite. "The tub," my dad called it, and it was about the size of a standard one. The basin collected water that warmed up more than the lake did and stayed clear to the bottom, even on cloudy days. The shells and rocks were easy to clear off the bottom to make sitting comfortable. When I was small, I would sit in the basin with my father whenever he took a rare break from work. We splashed in the water and laughed. It was a knowable place, but not entirely. The tub was adjacent to but apart from deeper parts of the lake, where the water kept its secrets.

In the mornings, when I was a bit older, I would go down to the tub and find freshwater mussel shells scattered across the rock edges. Evidence of raccoons, which, having grown up in the country, I never came to associate with garbage or aggression. I made a pet of one the summer my father found it crying beside its dead mother near the highway. He'd brought it home, and I fed it with a bottle. It would follow us around, reaching its small, wrinkled fingers up to be held. By August, though, it was too old for holding, and we trundled it into the small aluminum boat and motored down the lake, far from roads. The raccoon hopped out of the boat and ran straight into the trees, never looking back.

The rest of the lake remains a mystery to me. It is unfathomable, almost literally so in spots. Even though I lived beside it for decades, it is as enigmatic to me as it is intimate, and always it's the place in my mind where I go when I need to calm down. To ground myself. Strange, perhaps, to go to water for grounding. Then again, maybe an encounter with strangeness is what I am chasing. Maybe that's why I return, raccoon-like, to certain writings year after year. Like Freud and his fascinations with the strangeness that feels like but isn't quite home. Or Duras and her strange insights. Duras, who calls mothers the craziest people a child will ever know. When I think of myself as a mother, this is somewhat true. When I think of my own mother, it is also a bit true. It's almost unsettling how my mother's strangeness is repeated, somehow, in me.

* * *

In *The Uncanny*, which I love, Sigmund Freud tries to unknit the knotty question of provocation. Specifically, he's fixated on the provocation of feelings that are contradictory at their core: why do we feel both familiar and unnerved by certain things and people? Never mind for the moment that Freud uses as his example the story of "Der Sandmann" by E.T.A. Hoffmann, which, in its panoply of weird characters, settles on an automaton as a central example of uncanniness. Instead, consider Freud defining the uncanny as "a class of the terrifying which leads back to something long known to us, once very familiar." That is to say, the uncanny is an experience of confronting "the unknown in something you once thought knowable." It is a kind of mistake deep in the bottomless lake of the psyche. When you are about to make a mistake of this kind, there is a pricking up of the senses. Georges Bataille called this *horripilation*, literally the hair standing up in terror, but I think of it as the animal part of me on its hind legs, holding as still as possible and sniffing the air for a sign.

Hoffmann's tale is wild and complex. A haunted young man falls in love with an aloof young woman he spots in a window. He is besotted, while everyone around him is confused by her robotic affects. She is, in fact, an automaton, and the young man's slip into madness is attributed to being fooled by her makers. She is too real. But Freud suspected something more was going on. He wondered whether the young man's fall into insanity happens not at the realization that he was fooled, but at the realization that the fantasy of life with a perfect machine was better than an imperfect life with a fallible human. Gullibility is traded for madness and the strange, and when that strangeness is removed, the young man is bereft of meaning.

* * *

For two decades, my own mother inhabited a strangeness that I am trying, still, to unravel. As soon as Gull Lake was warm enough, my mother would go swimming early in the morning. But *early* doesn't quite capture it. She woke at 4:45 a.m., pulled on her bathing suit and goggles, and walked down to the lake. For years, this involved climbing over rocks slick with algae, before my father put in a dock built with materials recycled from a great-aunt and great-uncle's Airstream trailer porch. The water is about waist deep when you step into it from the dock, and then it drops down sharply ten feet. A little farther on, it drops farther still. Like all the lakes in the area—and there are many—this one is the result of glaciers passing through. It has crevasses and depths that confound the fish finders on the boats of the mostly American tourists who come for the bass. In the daylight, the lake is a mossy green colour. At night, it is black, and it is into this black version of the water my mother slipped and swam. For nearly an hour, in a darkness pitch-thick and viscous, she swam. A cloche of black, a blanket of black. A galaxy reflected on the surface of the lake not yet chopped up by the day's coming boats. Sometimes, as a younger child, I thought I could hear her from my room—door open for a crack of light, window open to catch a breeze—surely I could hear the soft one-two-three-breathe of her front crawl? But if I'm honest, I only imagined waking to listen.

One morning, after several years of this daily routine, there was an incident. I was asleep when it happened, but I imagine it like this: my mother is slicing steadily through the still-black water with her arms. There is a halo of morning light glowing above the trees. The water, still cold from its cover of night, creates a mist that hovers above the surface. I wonder if she can feel the mist as she swims. Through this comes the rumble of a motor, slow but steady, and then the sharp prow of a boat. The boat was a big one, and my mother small, and so its pilot didn't see her. For a moment I imagine they moved side by side, two swimmers keeping time. But then it hit her. This part is hard to imagine, though I have tried. A large outboard motorboat and my aquiline mother grazing one another in the half-dark. A propeller, a limb, a head face-down in one-two-three-breathe concentration. They collided, and then somehow my mother slipped out of the water and onto the shore, shaken but unharmed in any visible way. What was harmed was her sense of autonomy, I think. The belief that she could cut her way through black water on the brink of morning without consequence. For a time, she kept her routine, but something had crept into the edges of her mind, and so she changed. Her actions settled further into a strangeness that was both familiar and terrifying in its unfathomableness.

I have read so many books and seen so many films wherein the inciting incidents hinge on a mother entering a body of water. Often, when she breaks the surface, she startles her daughter. Consider this, from Claudia Dey's novel *Heartbreaker*:

> The last time my mother took me down to the reservoir, I refused to go into it. It was the middle of the night, late

> September... I watched her from the shore as she did her circuit. From one end to the other, from one end to the other. There was always a circuit to be completed. There was no moon and I could barely make out her body. She stopped in the middle of the black water and called out, "Time me!"

What this mother is doing, and what this daughter witnesses, is not explicit. Rather, it is the strangeness and the ritual, the witness and the act, that bear remark. I wonder at this calculus in the same moment I recognize it. Woman (usually mother) + significant and sinister body of water = what? A wavering? A wave? For the women always wave. There is Jane Campion's film *The Piano* in which the mother chooses for one moment to go with her beloved instrument into the sea, but then chooses to swim back to the surface. Or *The Queen's Gambit*, that miniseries about a chess-genius-orphan named Beth, who, in a key character-informing flashback, forms a sense of her own bright self while watching her terrifying and brilliant mother surface in the middle of a lake. Surface, smile, wave.

* * *

Shortly after my daughter was born, I received a message from my editor reminding me that I owed her. Of course, she didn't put it like that, but I did owe her, or rather, the press for which she edited. Not long before, I'd signed a contract to write a book of an undetermined length and, in my mind, on an impossibly important subject. I'd been pregnant and unemployed and, there's no other way to say it, drowning in unknowns. So I'd said yes, I could write the thing, and I'd signed the paper and cashed the advance to pay some bills, then I'd shoved the contract in a drawer. Was this a form of hubris? Perhaps.

When I was up at night nursing this small creature, I tallied my debts. I owed money. I owed writing. I was sure I didn't have the cash for either. The advance had been small—I was a first-time writer, a gamble at best—and the debts from school and years of precarious work were significant. *Milk money,* I sometimes thought to myself, child on my breast, and while it didn't really make sense, the phrase pushed back the edges of my fear for a moment. But the fear always came back, inky, thick, claustrophobic. I worried I was feeding my child this fear, but always when she was finished, she would unlatch and snuffle contentedly to sleep, unwavering in her calm.

* * *

After the boat incident, my mother became more extreme in her strange purposes. To her bathing suit, she strapped a foam bodyboard with an orange pylon affixed on top of it. On the pylon flashed a light meant for cycling after dark. For a long while, she also sported a fluorescent baseball cap, worn backwards, which was finally discarded when it faded from eye-searing yellow to white and then to what-was-once-white. Her route also changed. No more slow steps over roots and rocks to the water in front of the house. Instead, she walked down the driveway onto a secondary road, past the wooden bridge that her father and uncle had nearly burned down when they set off fireworks in the late 1950s, and into a farther, smaller lake. Round Lake. This lake is dark yellow-brown in the daylight. At night, it disappears into the shore, the blackness of the water connecting with the blackness of the woods in an unbroken line. On the far end of the lake, near a culvert, there is a hand-lettered sign painted on chipboards, affixed by my late grandfather to an inner tube, that reads *No Outboard Motors*.

I tried to go with her once. I realize now that I was in awe of my mother, and this made me competitive. I was also deep in the throes of teenage disgust—for myself, for my body, for things that felt beyond me and unnameable—and swimming struck me as pragmatic. Something I could get out of the way and brag about later. So up I got, and out the door I went carrying my own bodyboard and towel. The walk was cool and quiet. The stars were ostentatious. Sleep seeped out of my body with each step. My mother carried a flashlight, which was for my benefit. The light, steady in her hand, was a beacon of ordinariness against the curtain of unknowable dark. As if the beam were saying, "See? Just us walking down a dark road together." I said nothing but was grateful.

I could not make myself get into the water, despite my stubbornness. There was something about the bottomlessness of it, how everything that touched the water lost its edges. The small feral part of me bent on self-preservation held still. I wavered. I couldn't dip more than a toe in. There, on the edge of the lake, I could not get in. I waved to my mother, who was already several strokes out. She did not see me. I walked home with the flashlight, a little beacon, leaving her to stay afloat atop an endless and unplumbable drop.

* * *

One of the places Freud falters as he tries to name the feeling of unfamiliar familiar, of home that is no longer home-like, is around the mother's body. He can't quite get his words to work well. Those feelings that were once experiences are a waterway straight back to a source. The source is mother. The Mother. As if there were a single figure that fits us all the same.

What a ridiculous, limited notion. When I think of The Mother as an idea, as a lodestar, as my mother swimming under stars, I recall the ludicrous proposal by an earlier federal government to build a huge statue of "Mother Canada" facing out to sea, wistfully willing all her dead servicepeople home. During an interview on CBC, a Cape Bretoner put a pin in that fantasy when, questioned about his thoughts on the monument, he replied, "All we see is the arse-end of her." That mother is not my mother and that mother is not me. But perhaps that is what happens when some of us lose our waterways, and suddenly all of life has clear lines and hard edges and arranges itself *just so* on the shelf. A particular mother becomes The Mother. An idea. An ideal. An arse-end. A set of expectations to bash heads against. Freud wished for the mother to be the site of the uncanny because her body was once known to him. But mothers are swift, it seems. Swift and strange and fathomless, despite the desires pinned to their backs.

* * *

All through my pregnancy, I swam. I swam and I avoided deadlines. I swam in a pool at the university where I worked part-time. Most days, the lanes were shortened, and I slipped into the water with ease, moving back and forth with a speed that shocked the older swimmers who would appear on their lunch breaks. Not because I was fast, but because I was pregnant and lap swimming. Back and forth. Back and forth. I stopped for water every fifteen laps. I kept this up almost until the day my daughter was born. I kept it up well past the point of being able to do anything after the swim, not even my work. Under water, time shifted. Underwater, my mind softened its grip on the impossible future, all the unknowns I was growing. Underwater, my terror couldn't reach me, so I swam. One, two, three, breathe.

It turns out that the circuit-swimming mother of *Heartbreaker* has her own reasons for her mad acts. "Night became my mother's time," her daughter tells us. "She could wander. Night didn't ask anything of her. It did not shame her." Or, I'd add, pin her down.

In the end, I wrote that first book for my new small girl who made time bend. I wrote in hours snatched from the margins of my life. "The blue hours," Sylvia Plath called them. "That still, blue, almost eternal hour before cockcrow, before the baby's cry, before the glassy music of the milkman, settling his bottles." I wrote in a froth of possibility. There was nothing between my thinking, my fingers, the keyboard, except the watchful gaze of the dog. Writing, I told my partner, brought me back to myself.

* * *

Freud ends his essay on the uncanny sounding exhausted, which I appreciate. After the avalanche of etymological unpacking, after the analysis of Hoffmann's strange story, with its wide-eyed automatons and vision-stealing monsters, Freud returns to the realm of the aesthetic. He returns to the scene of writing. Writing, Freud surmises, is the province of the uncanny. It is perhaps most obvious in stories where the writer wants the reader to feel fear and foreboding. To feel their own little lives watched by some indefinite creature, just off-scene or staring up from the depths. This is the province of the writer—to conjure the strangeness of living and render it palpable, if only for a sentence or two. But this, against all the rules of strong essay writing, is not where Freud lands. Instead, as though he cannot help himself, he leaves the reader with this impossible sentence: "Concerning the factors of silence, solitude, and darkness, we can only say that there are actually elements in the production of that infantile morbid anxiety from which the majority of human beings have never become quite free." While his phrasing stinks of the desire to make medical that which is not, I still like this because I recognize it, at least in part. There are echoes here of Duras's claim about mothers and their strangeness.

And now, years into my own mothering, I recognize the pleasure of strangeness differently. When I look into what seems an impossible calculus of silence, solitude, and darkness, I see those strange numbers slipping into place. Most mornings, in my own blue hours, I creep down the stairs of my home in the darkness while the sleepers sleep. The hours I keep make sense to me alone. Imperfectly, daily, I feel my childhood stretch both further from me and, uncannily, sidle up and slip beneath my arm. Each morning, in the reach for wakefulness, for the different inhabitation of the water of my mind, I swim further into myself. Alone, or perhaps in company with the strange makings of other mothers. I understand my own mother's morning rituals better from here. What may appear strange or boring from any other vantage has become, for me, repetitious and peaceful ordinariness. I have circled back to the beginning. My own uncanny return not to the dark depths of the lake of my actual childhood, but to a ritual space apart but not severed from my own mothering. Silence. Solitude. Darkness. Waters I relish swimming in, for a small time, daily.

ON STYLE AS SURVIVAL

She fortified herself against the dismalness of this... by various small indulgences. Out of these she had contrived for herself a mental fur coat.
Sylvia Townsend Warner

Of the people in the world who have experienced high school, there are two distinct groups: those for whom it was the best time in their lives, and those for whom it was an exercise in perseverance. I am in the latter group. For me, high school meant listening to Nirvana and yearning to be part of the Riot Grrrl movement in a place where Tim McGraw ruled the airwaves. My peers were the characters from *90210,* and I wished I was an extra on *My So-Called Life*.

I had moved to rural North Carolina with my parents at the start of middle school, a place small enough that almost all the kids had known each other since birth. My small school housed grades one through twelve and sat on a hill in the middle of a horse pasture. The only change high school brought was that we moved to the opposite end of the school building. I wasn't bullied in high school but had been earlier. By high school, I had some good acquaintances, did reasonably well in classes, and played soccer and volleyball relatively competently. I was biding my time. I did not have a sense of belonging either to the place or to the people in it. I had, instead, a kind of fidelity to my own ordinary strangeness. I was also in possession of a 1989 Oldsmobile Cutlass Ciera.

Driving was freedom. I got my "beginners" license at fifteen, and I purchased the maroon car the minute I turned sixteen. It had low milage thanks to its first owner, who was elderly and lived in town. The car cost seven thousand American dollars, all of which I'd saved from jobs washing dishes and serving old men their morning coffee. I did not care that the Oldsmobile was second-hand, that its style signalled age. I cared that the trunk was big enough to fit a pony keg and the front seat was a bench. I cared that the tape deck worked; I had an adaptor for my CD player. My mother gave me a phone in a bag to plug into the cigarette lighter for emergencies and a small can of pepper spray. She was freed from driving me thirty miles to school, and I was free to play whatever I wanted on the blown-out speakers while I ferried myself along the back roads of Warren County.

What can I tell you about the drive to school? It was long, its own kind of durational practice. It was also beautiful. Down our gravel drive, nearly half a mile, past the small and struggling pear trees my father had planted the year we arrived. Left onto the road that used to be a main one but was now designated a rural route. Windows down to smell the honeysuckle in spring and the sweet, sticky smell of kudzu, advancing with its green train trailing over pine trees, telephone poles, and everything in its path. Past the low grey store with a corrugated metal roof and a faded Amoco sign out front. It wasn't the only store on the road to the highway, but it was the one people meant when they referred to "the store." The owner kept collard patches on the side, and anyone who needed could take some of the thick fanned leaves. Before I was old enough to own the Oldsmobile, I sometimes had to catch a ride to school with the neighbours, which meant stopping at the store each morning and waiting in the back seat while they tumbled out to get breakfast and three dollars of gas to get to town. Coca-Cola and Moon Pies, that's what they returned to the car with. The food of an unfamiliar place, only that place was here, and here, now, was home.

The Oldsmobile freed me from the stickiness of ride-sharing, the unfamiliar bickering of siblings, and back-seat nausea. It freed me from stopping at "the store." I preferred to buy my gas in town at the new station that had coffee and flavoured water in cans. These were small indulgences out of which I was contriving to build something for myself.

Just before the on-ramp for the interstate, I would pass a pink trailer that looked abandoned but wasn't. The trailer was positioned with its back toward the road to hide the cars parked in its U-shaped drive. Curtains always pulled. Lights always on inside. That trailer, and the work done there, was the first instance I recall of hearing a joke where a woman was the punchline. Just past this trailer, which was called the Pink Motel by men my father's age, was the good gas station with its Diet Dr Pepper and single Tootsie Rolls. I sometimes bought gas there just to imagine being elsewhere before pulling onto the interstate. I-85 is a major highway bordered by pines all the way from Alexandria, Virginia, down to nearly Montgomery, Alabama. The stretch I took into town was part of the Highway of Heroes, named for people who had died honourable deaths far away. When we first arrived, the road was strung with the yellow ribbons of the Gulf War. Many of those ribbons stayed for years, fading from yellow to beige to a shade that reminded me of skim milk.

Driving on this road required concentration and a kind of grit. Some days eighteen wheelers on their way to or from New York or Florida would box me in just for fun. The drivers would honk their horns, and I could see them talking to each other on their radios. The Oldsmobile was a little too tall to fit right underneath the trucks, but I thought of this happening often and wondered if I could manage such a feat of trick driving. The speed limit on I-85 is 65 miles per hour, which is a cool 104.6 kilometers an hour. It is neither too fast nor too slow, but no one drives that speed. Mostly, there were the trucks barreling into my rear-view mirror, or the lowriders moving at a slower pace to save their suspension. I turned up the music as loud as it would go and kept my eyes straight ahead at the horizon.

* * *

I've learned many things from the poet Joyelle McSweeney, including that at the end of a fable of endurance and survival, you have to report back on what you've learned. There is a responsibility in that genre to pay it forward. Magic does not call again if you don't share what you know. Of her own journey of survival, McSweeney says, "concern for style is not secondary to concern for survival. I learned that survival requires a style." Style, for her, isn't only a literary mode. Instead, style is a methodology for perseverance and endurance that weaves itself into survival as a state. In a poem on surviving the death of her infant child, McSweeney writes about the importance of her Vans sneakers and Marimekko robe, which wrap her grief in a kind of stylish force field. She perceives, too, the movement of a skunk as style embodied, then springboards these images—sneakers, robe, skunk—into an aesthetic method she names "death styles." Sometimes, survival wears a big floral print robe and skate shoes. Sometimes, it drives a 1989 sedan. Other times, survival is styled in a fur coat.

Along with the Oldsmobile, I relied on Janis Joplin's raspy voice and punk-rock spirit to lift me up and out of those solitary teenage years. While my classmates sang along to "Chattahoochee" through the open windows of so many Honda Civics, I drove myself home on the back roads with Janis's version of "Summertime" for company. Knowing that Gershwin hated what she'd done to his song only made me love it more. Her Southern Comfort–soaked voice wrapped me in a sense that there was a world beyond the horizon I could see.

In a photograph from 1969, Janis Joplin's right arm is raised high over her head. Below her hand, which is giving a peace sign, her wrist is filled with bracelets. She is smiling at photographers. Joplin, who is twenty-six in the photo, has just been released on bail from a prison in Tampa, Florida, where she had been held since her arrest the previous night. The charge was obscenity. Joplin had been told by police to quiet her audience, who were dancing in the aisles and standing on seats to see the show. Her response was to tell the police, "Don't fuck with these people."

In her mug shot, she is wearing a floor-length dress, but by the time she leaves the prison the next morning, her outfit is different: she is wearing a fur coat and fur hat in the Florida sun. Both are oversized. The hat wraps around her head like a cat, while the coat looks like it was made for being draped over things. Shoulders, chairs, banisters. A rebellious woman's mind in need of a buffer. I wonder about this fur coat, this stylish signal of survival. Had Joplin asked her lawyer, Herbert Goldburg, to bring it for her? Had a friend or a bandmate sifted through a chaotic tour bus to find it? Had someone brought it to her as a joke? I want to speak to the archivist of getting-out-of-prison outfits, because this fur coat is working double time. It is signifying abundance, affluence, comfort, a kind of separateness from the present moment. Seeing a photo of Joplin in that coat, smiling and giving a peace sign, was freedom personified. That photo made me feel like I was driving, windows down, hand surfing the air as the landscape passes to the rear-view. An Oldsmobile Cutlass Ciera. Death styles. A fur coat that says *Don't fuck with these people* but also warns not to fuck with the woman wearing it. All these things, which one might ungenerously want to see as small indulgences, are, in fact, specialist tools.

* * *

I think often of the phrase "a mental fur coat," which comes from a novel called *Lolly Willowes; or the Loving Huntsman*. You'd be forgiven if you haven't read the book or heard of its author, Sylvia Townsend Warner, for, though she was well-enough known in her day, she hasn't cast the same wide spell on readers as her contemporaries Virginia Woolf and Jean Rhys. Townsend Warner's work is not radical in its innovations of interiority or grammar. She isn't breaking the logic of the sentence, or rewiring the way a reader encounters gender through syntax, or writing back against gendered and colonial narratives with a pen on fire. Instead, with *Lolly Willowes*, Townsend Warner works at the edge of domestic realism—a genre in which novels revel in detail to tell it like it is, novels that twenty-first-century readers find excruciating or deliciously immersive, depending on their tastes. Inside the finely wrought cages of their own social mores, Townsend Warner's characters beat their wings without realizing they are being drawn further into their own entrapment. Except for Lolly.

Escaping the entrapment of the expectations projected onto her—those intelligible narratives—is no small feat. The novel opens with Lolly's condemnation to a life of service. The conditions of patriarchal structure are as plain as a door slamming shut: "When her father died, Laura Willowes went to live in London with her brother and his family. 'Of course,' said Caroline, 'you will come to us.'" Thus Laura, who will soon be called "Lolly" by a toddler nephew, has her fate yoked to guardianship. Well into her twenties when her father dies, her life is still not her own. She is an object, much like antique furniture or a taxidermied parrot, though a bit more difficult to manage. She is objectified through structures of duty and care. Her worth is measured in her capacity to ferry her nieces to dance classes or offer her rings to her toddler nephew to play with. She is all background noise and use value. Like the family heirlooms, she is a thing to be passed between households.

Let's sit momentarily with this stark detail of one woman, Lolly's sister-in-law Caroline, guaranteeing the captivity of another, and in so doing, reaffirming her own. Caroline's dutiful affirmative reveals her own entanglement in the regulation of women's agency. Obviously, Laura will go with Caroline. Obviously, she'll be bound for life to Caroline's benevolent dictatorship of pantries and parlours. Caroline's is a Christian generosity, the kind that binds and gags the recipient with gussied-up parsimony and passive-aggressive inferences to gratitude and callings. With her utterance—"of course"—Caroline consigns Laura to a lifetime of embroidery and quiet remarks, and the guarantee that she will slowly suffocate via unwanted and unappreciated duty to the systems and people within them who control her life. These two words—"of course"—lock the gate on Laura's freedom, and both Laura and Caroline know it.

The entrapment that Lolly experiences is often described in terms of hue, or rather, the absence of colour. Lolly herself is described as lacking. She is past pale, with grey eyes that are more a watered-down black than a true shade unto themselves. She is unremarkable, forgettable, fading into the upholstery as she waits for her nieces to finish dance lessons, or as she steps softly and unnoticed up the side stairs. She is wallpaper. She is a waning bloom who fades in front of the World War I recruitment posters, as she stands and resolutely packs box after box for the boys at the front. So good is she at this repetitive work that no one thinks to offer her another job, and Lolly, ever dutiful, doesn't make a fuss. She works herself nearly to death in the service of others, succumbing to the flu epidemic only when the end of the war is announced and her volunteer labour won't be missed. She waits to get sick, in other words, until her illness won't bother anyone.

Eventually, Lolly leaves her brother's house and radically reinvents her life in a place called Great Mop. But before she manages to leave, she spends years honing tactics of survival. Specifically, she fashions what she calls a "mental fur coat." This fur coat of Lolly's is an emotional shield between herself and the bother the world brings. This fur coat is figurative, unlike Joplin's statement garment, but the work is similar. Lolly's mental fur coat is the colour blue, and it can soothe eyes that are sore from lack of beauty. The mental fur coat has the same feeling as walking into a room already warmed by a fireplace. Her fur coat is a hand that reaches over with a brief, reassuring squeeze. Made of furtive rituals of pleasure, Lolly's mental fur coat keeps her from slipping off the drop edge of yonder into bottomless despair. She creates moments of pleasure and joy for herself in a life built on service to others. She buys flowers. She takes rest. She eats marron glacé alone. Lolly's rituals are minor, not obviously revolutionary. But the point of a fur coat isn't revolution. The point of the fur coat—of style, here—is survival. It is getting by. It is buffering yourself from the world's freezing unfairness however you can. And Lolly's small rituals are enough to keep her warm.

Warner published *Lolly Willowes* three years before Virginia Woolf published *A Room of One's Own*. Unlike Woolf's non-fiction, Warner's exploration of the limitations and expectations placed on women is a work of fabulation. Still, there are some uncanny similarities. In the early decades of the twentieth century, unmarried women did have choices, though they were not particularly expansive, especially for women who did not come from wealthy families. But capital and class create their own cascading set of cages. Having money might soften the world for a few people, but it does not eradicate the system in which we all punch the clock. Power and privilege are foot soldiers for the voraciousness of interconnected systems of oppression. Woolf had at least a teaspoon of both power and privilege, and still she was denied entry at the library door. Lolly had privilege in her family's wealth and solid position in the brutal matrix of British middle-class whiteness, and still she was stuck, consigned to an existence of responding to the needs of others and relegating her own wishes to a dark cupboard of the soul. Money can do many things, but it is imbricated in capitalism—it is the actor for the system's ill logic—and so it will always limit what is possible on a larger scale. That's another trap: the notion that if we perform our individuality well enough, we will somehow be recognized as exceptional and be granted escape from these stultifying systems.

Are Lolly's furtive rituals a version of my generation's "li'l treats"? Maybe. The bigger question is whether they are short-term fixes for bigger problems. The mental fur coat and the rituals of pleasure it hails remind me of Hannah Arendt, who warned us to be aware of falling too far into small pleasures. Bear with me. There is a phrase in French—petit bonheur—which translates to "small happiness." On its own, the phrase is a reminder to revel in quotidian delight. Hands wrapped around a pottery mug filled with hot coffee. Catching sight of a bird landing on a branch outside the window. A corner of the couch made more inviting with soft lighting and a colourful quilt. But Arendt was writing in the late 1940s, amidst the occupation of France by Nazis. In Vichy France, delighting in small pleasures usually took place in the home, cloistered from the collapsing public sphere. Arendt diagnosed the rise in petite bonheur as a symptom of that collapse. People turned away from the cacophony and violence of the public sphere and turned toward the small and private sphere of the home. Arendt predicted that the amplification of the private would come at a cost. How can one care about the world and the creatures in it if you're too busy cultivating coziness?

More recent writers have compared the tenderness of presenting our private spheres online—especially in the Covid-19 pandemic—with a kind of doubling down on petit bonheur. I think about this now when I feel the pull of comparison while scrolling. Can I curate my life with antique baskets and neutral linens too? Should I? I think also of the ways that carving out space for the self to unfurl without surveillance is something quite different and rare. Small pleasure as survival; I also learned that from reading Audre Lorde. A mental fur coat won't protect you from the ways that life, modern or otherwise, can drain the colour and oxygen, diminishing the wild possibilities of solidarity from everyday life. But it might just give you the fortitude to continue.

* * *

Janis Joplin was not the only woman to navigate scrutiny while in furs, not by a long shot. Twenty years before Joplin's exuberant jailhouse exit, Billie Holiday was photographed signing court documents in a police station in San Francisco. Her hotel room had been raided on a premise—suspicion of narcotics use—and so off Holiday was taken, down to the station, draped in mink.

Billie Holiday's fur coat is longer than Joplin's. The sleeves are wider, too. In the photo I've seen, Holiday isn't facing the camera; she is focused on signing those legal papers. Her diamanté sunglasses are on, and her hair is swept back under an elegant headwrap. She's wearing earrings that appear to be diamond crescent moons, but I can't be sure. Her nails are painted a dark colour, and she's holding her purse as well as the paperwork. Her 1949 arrest was built around Holiday's known narcotics use, but the real aim of it was to shut her up. She'd been singing "Strange Fruit," and the FBI didn't like that. "Strange Fruit" is an anti-lynching song that wields the full power of metaphor to condemn violent and genocidal anti-Black agendas in America. The song was written by schoolteacher and poet Abel Meeropol, who presented it to Holiday in 1939. Meeropol's metaphors are crucial, but it's Holliday's vocal stylings that give the song its revolutionary force. When Holliday sang "Strange Fruit," the harvest of white supremacy was served to the white people who'd paid to see Lady Day perform. Holiday's arrangements were as eminently dazzling as they were technically accomplished. A pedagogue of hard truths, she taught people with flowers in her hair.

Much has been written about Holiday's personal style—vocal and self-presentation. How her insistence on gowns, gardenias, sunglasses, and, of course, the fur coat, was more than just fashion. Insisting on looking good, on accessing the signification powers of affluence, flew in the face of racist gaslighting and tacit (or not so tacit) suggestions that some things were for white people, full stop. You can't arrest a person for killer style, but there are other ways to clip her wings. That's what the machine of white America knew.

What I see is fur coat as survival style. Maybe Holliday wore that fur coat as a visual manifestation of refusal. Perhaps her style is a tactic that teaches insurgent strategies, a kind of magic conjuring of a future more beautiful than her ruthless present. Kathy Acker used to say, "If it can't be done, but it must be done, then it will be done, by magic." Holiday—in the court lobby, in her furs—doing the magic that must be done to survive the blasted present handed to her. Perhaps the fur coat is a code that bypasses the censors of survival to reach readers in need of a small solidarity.

Let's try this: the point of any mental fur coat is to index a sense of survival, though what needs surviving is uneven, to be sure. This is about the need to survive in the face of the relentless bother that social norms will bring to your doorstep and drop in your lap. McSweeney writes,

> Style is a recognition of things which are like us, and which we would like to be like. In this sense, style is simulacra—the copy, the double, that allows art to be made, that *is* Art, both a display and self-encryption that allows us to survive life's plot.

A mental fur coat hangs in the space between boredom and bother. Before or after overt acts that require survival—exiting a jail cell, demanding that people be unfucked with—the mental fur coat insulates the wearer. There are moments when the furtive ritual can become a bridge to somewhere else. Lolly's mental fur coat insulated her from her leaching present and enabled her first furtive steps out of London, toward Great Mop and a whole new life. Imagine that. Slow resistance built over time.

* * *

Where we lived in North Carolina, out in the country, where the houses were few and far between, I learned it wasn't safe for a girl to walk alone. Yet I craved solitude and agency. I was ravenous for magic and adventure of my own making. Getting in the driver's seat of the Oldsmobile was delicious. It felt like slipping the future tense around my shoulders. Inside that car, I wasn't just safe; I was insulated. From the world. From being stuck at a bad party. I had a room of my own with doors that locked and four wheels that would take me down any highway or gravel road. In my car, I could control everything from the atmosphere to the soundtrack to the speed. I wrapped myself in that car not just to survive but also to edit my own life's plot. Here is an off-ramp. Here is a different road. Perhaps a car is also a fur coat, depending on how it is worn.

There is a final photo that, for me, holds all these perhapses and fashions them into something stylish, too. In a photograph of Nina Simone, taken in the lobby of the Dorchester Hotel in London in 1998, the High Priestess of Soul is seated. She is wearing an enormous, lush fur coat. She holds her oversized purse on her lap, and she is staring directly at the camera. She has declined to smile. By this time, Simone would have been sixty-five. She had left America more than a decade prior, sick of its failures, and instead made the world her home. Apparently, she has just finished saying to the photographer, "Take the damn picture." She has already written and performed, time and again, "Mississippi Goddam" and "Four Women." She has refashioned "Trouble in Mind" to make it hers. She and Billie and Janis each vocalized "Summertime," and in doing so changed it to centre their own longings. Simone has already moved through indignities and violence into protest and action. She has reserved some of herself for herself. Her style is written into every contour of her face and every angle of her posture. And there she sits, in her gorgeous fur coat, staring the camera and its man down.

ON COLLISION AND WITNESS

I was born in 1979. That was the year the Government of Quebec hired a French theorist to write a report about the state of culture. The theorist was Jean-François Lyotard, and the report was *The Postmodern Condition: A Report on Knowledge*. Written at the request of the Conseil des universités du Québec to track the influence of technology on the exact sciences, the report suggests that the postmodern condition can be characterized by what Lyotard calls an "incredulity towards metanarratives." At a most basic interpretation, he means that the big stories that give people guardrails on their lives are no longer enough. God, government, capital: none of it could keep us in line anymore, at least not intellectually. Without the presence of a capital-T Truth, a sense of gravitational pull and purpose had disappeared. Belief had to happen through a sheer force of madness or will, nothing more. Trajectories, linear progress, all of it had proven to be more complex and random than we'd initially thought, if not totally rigged. And so, Lyotard surmised, we were, from at least 1979, finding our ways without clear stories of meaning to keep us on our paths.

There was a lot going on in the 1970s, etymologically. When is there not a lot going on, etymologically? While the word *collision* shows up in English in the 1600s, it really gets going several hundred years later. Collision's roots are Latinate and mean "to strike or dash together forcibly." The term has stayed in popular usage since its arrival, but there is a marked uptick in usage in the late 1970s. Worlds, markets, ideologies, narratives, bodies, objects. Everyone was subject to a forcible dashing together in a way that suddenly seemed to have a narrative arc. We still are.

* * *

Fifteen years ago, when I moved from the middle of the country to the edge of the Atlantic, I bought a bicycle. It was cherry red with white zigzags around the branding. It made me think of electricity. The handlebars were low and felt dangerous, like whoever rode it was not a force to be reckoned with. I bought cycling shoes with clips on the bottoms and learned to kick my heel out to release my foot from where it would lock into the pedal. This was a bicycle for a serious cyclist, and while I wasn't one yet, I had a feeling I could be.

As it turned out, the city I moved to made no room for cyclists. Vehicles would honk or edge me into parked cars as I made my way from one place to another. The roads had no shoulders to speak of, and there was little room for error. Some might take this lack of space as a challenge and petition the city for infrastructure or, like the couriers I knew, develop a passion for punching the side mirrors off cars that came too close. I chose instead to limit my cycling to the countryside, where the bicycle delivered on its promise of freedom and expansiveness. I rode into places that had patchy cell service. Nothing could reach me.

When our child learned to ride her own bicycle, her joy was also effervescent. After weeks of wobbly starts and spectacular slow-motion crashes, there she went, off on her own two wheels. I jogged after her but quickly fell behind. What is a cliché when it is also arresting? There went my heart, bombing exuberantly around the park pathways that loop through the Commons. She zoomed ahead, hair streaming out from beneath her little red helmet.

Long after the Oldsmobile was retired, my red bicycle served as my co-conspirator. Together, we moved my body and my fluctuating moods around the province. My favourite place to ride was along the Northumberland Strait, where woods meet fields meet ocean. My bicycle and I swooped across all of it. Some mornings, moving on well-oiled gears, I would surprise a deer. Once, a figure I thought was an older man stooping down in the ditch straightened to reveal the sloped shoulders of a yearling black bear. These encounters made my heart race, but they did not scare me. On the contrary, they felt almost sacred.

When we spent weekends away from the city, I would sometimes use errands as an excuse to get out and pedal. Occasionally, though, I wouldn't sleep well, and I'd fail to overcome my inertia. One such morning, ruing my laziness and rubbing my eyes, I made the ten-kilometre drive to the nearest store to get milk. The road is a secondary highway that runs along the red-sand coast.

Deborah Levy suggests that animating affect is a useful experience because it draws edges around a nameless, faceless feeling. She doesn't put it quite like that, though. Instead, she depicts fear as a jaguar that stalks one of her characters as she moves around Berlin. The fear-jaguar is lithe, wily, powerful. The woman always feels the jaguar before she sees it. I swear I felt my own jaguar somewhere nearby as I crested the small hill just before the store and sensed that something wasn't right. I slowed the car to a crawl. A few people were moving quickly toward a van facing the wrong way in the opposite ditch. I rolled down my windows, pulled into the store's gravel parking lot, and got out of my car. I felt aware of my hands and was unsure what to do with them. A woman ran from the store to the van with a beach towel that was bright pink and orange. Everything was quiet, as if sound had been muted. A different woman was then helped out of the van by a large man in a baseball cap. That was when the screaming started. The sound was so guttural I looked around for an animal. I assumed a dog had been maimed, until I saw the bicycle wheel. It was partway under the car and still spinning slowly. Three early-morning cyclists pulled up beside me and dismounted. Together we watched. We did not speak.

I imagine now that what I was thinking about was the number twenty-one, but I know that came later. Twenty-one grams is the supposed amount of weight a body loses after a person dies. Dr. Duncan MacDougall conducted an experiment that led to this discovery in 1907, when tuberculosis was rampant. First, he weighed six different patients in their final stages of succumbing to the disease. After they each died, he weighed them again. Each was twenty-one grams lighter, and so he surmised that was the heft of a human soul.

21 Grams is also the name of a film starring Naomi Watts. I think about that film often, but what I don't like to think about is how the fact of this measurement was discovered. The premise of the film is both philosophical and banal: what happens when life changes in an instant? The banality comes in the rear-view—life is always changing in a series of instants. What is captivating is how the narrative engages with the business of rendering the effects of instants into story. There are three interconnected tales that do this work. Watts's character has just lost her husband and two daughters in a hit and run. Sean Penn plays a mathematician with heart failure who received Watts's husband's heart after he's killed. Benicio del Toro is a criminal whose erratic behaviour sets the action in motion; he spends the film haunted by the repercussions of his actions. I grew up in church and while there was much talk of souls and how they might be lost, I couldn't name a single time their weight was mentioned. If you acted right and prayed diligently, yours would be well cared for. That's what I knew. But I also wondered what would happen if you died right in the middle of figuring things out.

It was clear the cyclist had not survived the impact. The barometric pressure of the morning shifted just a little. My hands started shaking so hard that I kept dropping my keys. The early-morning cyclists were standing as still as deer who've just heard the sound of stalking. I turned away from them and walked into the store. I bought bread and almond milk for our friend who was visiting. I bought hand soap and chocolate milk and a bag of potato chips. I considered lavender mosquito spray but left it on the shelf. I walked back to the car and sat in the front seat and opened the chips. They were delicious and salty and for a moment I couldn't believe I lived in a world where chips exist. Then the shaking moved from my hands to my whole body. I sat there watching the cyclists, hands on their low-slung handlebars, shifting from foot to foot, bearing witness.

There is a scene in Doris Betts's novel *Souls Raised from the Dead* in which the protagonist, a highway patrol officer in North Carolina, arrives at the scene of an accident. The crash is a bad one, the driver has clearly not survived. But when the patrol officer shines his flashlight into the cracked back window, the beam of light finds a child, and that child is looking back at him. Frank, that's the patrol officer's name, had just lost his own child some months before. Not in a crash, but from the crush of living in a body susceptible to heredity and disease. The book ends with Frank driving to the hospital again, this time to check on the child from the crash. Someone else's daughter, this one saved.

* * *

"Why is Truro always like this?"

The words left my mouth and then the world exploded.

We had been sitting in traffic on Highway 102, like always. It is inexplicable to me why road work happens when it does on Friday afternoons or long weekends. This particular stretch of construction felt like money laundering. Every summer like clockwork the highway part of a little overpass outside of Truro, Nova Scotia, is limited to one lane. It's hard to say what work is actually being accomplished, though there are many machines and just as many workers. We were on our way to the funeral of my partner's grandmother. She'd made it to a century, which was a feat. Still, any departure is significant, and we were feeling heavy.

I had meant it as a joke, my question about the town we were driving through. We weren't in a hurry, and we were used to the three-hour trip. Our child was in the back seat chatting as we took turns choosing songs to play. Once we passed Truro, we would let her watch a program with her headphones on, and my partner and I would talk, or be silent, or listen to music that only we two had to agree on. The dog was asleep with his huge head on our child's lap. I was trying to make my partner laugh. Making fun of Truro remains a long-running, lighthearted joke between us. When I was pregnant, we'd agreed that if I went into labour on the drive to or from his mother's house, about two hours from our home in Halifax, we'd just press on in either direction to avoid the Truro hospital.

When I opened my eyes after the roar of smoke and sound, I couldn't tell if seconds or minutes had passed. The world was grey and fuzzy, and loud sirens were coming at us from at least two directions. There were parachutes pressing on me from all sides, and at first I couldn't find our child. The dog was shuddering—he had been thrown from the back seat to the front and lay crumpled against the dash.

We had, of course, been hit from behind. The parachutes were airbags, and I couldn't find our daughter because we'd been hit so hard that my seat collapsed backward and it was leaning back on top of her. In addition to the sirens, I could hear a cool mechanical voice repeating something in stereo. I learned later that our phones, triangulating sound and velocity, had determined we'd been in a severe crash and had called 911.

The voice was my telephone telling an operator over and over where to find our car.

Somehow, we got out. The smoke that was pouring into the car through the vents made me certain the engine was on fire. Our girl, shaking from head to toe and unable to speak, crawled out of the car and stood in her socks in a puddle. I found her shoes in different parts of the wreckage, knocked from her feet by the impact. My partner was already out of the car. He'd tell me later that he was so sure he'd find the person who hit us halfway through their own windshield that he ran to be with them and shield our daughter from the sight. Instead, he found a man crawling through his sunroof, shaken but alive.

The rest of it is a blur. Cars crawling by on one side, racing on the other. Rain. A stranger holding paper towel to my face and explaining that my nose was bleeding. A woman who walked across traffic to hold our child's hand and lead us to a quieter place on the grass. The normally exuberant dog shaking silently beside me. The firefighters checking our pupils and our pulses. Police confusing me by being tender. Our first time in the back seat of a cruiser. The long wait to be picked up, only to continue back on the highway the rest of the way to my mother-in-law's house. The hospital visits, like the bruises and scabs, would come later.

* * *

I love to walk. The older I get, the more I relish the incredible feeling of moving from one place to another. Thinking loosens when I move, as though feelings and inarticulate ideas lodge themselves in corners of my being and only movement can pry them free. After coming across the cycling accident, I gave away my red bicycle. Walking and running became my freedom, and I clung to them as fiercely as I once had to my handlebars.

Months after I witnessed the aftermath of the bike accident, and weeks after our own car crash, we lost a friend. More than a friend, really. She had been the kind of friend you call not just to celebrate with cake and champagne, but also for help with the mundane and the gritty. She and her partner lived across the street from us, and during the Covid-19 pandemic lockdown months we would sit on our respective stoops and have dinner together. She was my first friend when I got my permanent job teaching at the university. She was the kind of person you immediately want to be around. Luminous. Caring. Brilliant. An incredibly silly goose.

In the previous year, though, she had gone silent. Moved herself away across the country with a casual wave, promising to return refreshed. Instead, she quietly managed a devastating diagnosis and left this plane on her own terms. I found out a few hours after she'd gone. We were bereft, but that's the thing—it wasn't our choice to make, and now all we could do was choose how to apprehend the loss of her. That's what we told our child, at any rate. Me, I walked. I chose nothing but motion as I ricocheted between deep grief and a white-hot anger. Walking was, for a while, the only thing that helped.

That was how I found myself watching a stranger and the police. I'd been walking, thinking about my dead friend, trying to understand why she'd left without telling us. Without telling me. I had covered a class for a colleague who was ill, so it was later than usual when I started walking home from the university. Even though I am middle-aged, I still skip the shortcut through the dark graveyard and instead walk its perimeter, where the road runs between the graveyard and the hospital. It was from there that I watched a man run screaming across the road, away from a row of parked cars. I watched two officers run after him and grab him as he kicked and windmilled his arms and wailed. I couldn't tell what he was saying, but it sounded like both a lament and a curse. A name or a phrase. As much as I was disoriented by what I was seeing, I also badly wanted to understand what was happening.

There is a common feeling when you realize something is there with you in a room. A sense of being perceived that creeps up on you like a flush. I think, now, that was the pull that made me turn from the melee and look across the road. There, both arms at right angles, like a toddler in deep sleep, I saw a young person beneath a car. The scene was so wrong it scrambled my brain. I could not translate what I was seeing into good sense. What was this serene young person doing resting under the car, arms raised as though in surrender? Who were all those people on the sidewalk? Should I help? Could I?

Neither this young person nor our friend was alone when they left this place. There had been witnesses. I was a witness. And yet I did not know what to make of this huge responsibility. What I do know is that the shaking came faster this time and didn't stop, not even after my partner came to get me and I was tucked in my own house with my arms around our big dog's neck.

* * *

We were sitting at the bar of the second-best coffee shop in town, my friend and I. Amid the bangs and muted screams of the barista's machine, my friend, who is a poet, looked me in the eye. She was about as serious as I had seen her. I did not care for this. It's hard to shift in your seat when your seat is a barstool, and so I recrossed my ankles at a different angle.

"You have to stop and ask what it wants," my friend said. "You need to go somewhere quiet, clear your mind of all the buzz, and say to it, 'What are you, what do you need?' and 'Why are you chasing me?' And then you need to listen."

My friend was probably onto something. In six months, I had seen two people die, nearly lost myself and my family in a car crash, had a close friend pass suddenly, and been on two different flights with medical emergencies. I was feeling more than a little haunted.

In terms of spiritual training, mine is of the punitive sort. The kind of higher power that watches and waits for you to make an error. You mess up, you're marked by it. Mine is not a lineage with the possibility of confession. Shame is a thing you wear, an emotional hair shirt that bothers the edges of your being. The suggestion that I was somehow being shadowed by something I couldn't see was bad enough, but the suggestion that I could acknowledge it and greet it and work with it was altogether beyond. I wasn't equipped for this. What's more, I didn't want to do it. What I wanted was freedom, I thought, though from what I couldn't say.

"The problem you're having," another friend explained, "is one of belief." She was telling me about how after she'd been hit by a car, she'd lost her sense of truth. It wasn't until a therapist explained her loss of belief that she understood why.

The social contract means that while the animal parts of us are aware of the danger around us, we tell ourselves stories so we can go about our days anyway. Get into a car and trust we'll get to our destination. Clip into our bike pedals and say, "See you soon." Step into a crosswalk and trust the cars will stop. After my friend was hit, she explained, it was like a veil had been pulled away from the storytelling part of her. She was incredulous. The narrative of living had let her down. "You feel it too, now." She held my hand as she said this. Not a curse, but not *not* a curse, either.

Let's imagine both these friends are onto something; let's imagine that what's tailing me has to do with both belief and witness. Witness, I suggest, because I don't know what else to do with all these collisions, departures, and near misses. I don't have a grand narrative for why I've witnessed so many people die. People who were vital to their circles. I don't have a good story for why our friend went away and never returned, or why some people get saved while many don't, or why my family landed in the "saved" group. What I do have is the suspicion that to witness things happening with care matters. To watch what happens and to be altered by it also matters. To try to record experiences with a poet's eye and a storyteller's sense of justice matters. If the jaguar that stalks the ordinary instances of a life wants something from me, let me witness it and work to get it down on paper before that big black cat appears, famished. Let me be brave, at least, and turn to face the fierce creature, lock eyes, and ask what it needs.

ON LOOKING AND LOOKING

I have three photos open on my computer screen. I made copies of the photos and placed them deliberately on my desktop. To view them, I have to click on each one, arrange the photos so I can see all three at once, and move my eyes between them. There is almost a century between their composition, but between them is a link I feel but struggle to name. Somehow, triangulated together on my screen, they *almost* answer a question about how care happens across time. The photos feel urgent. Their site of affiliation is now. What I mean is, I am drawn to them daily. If I look hard enough, perhaps the link will reveal itself more clearly. If I can give my attention to the stories these photos hold for long enough, perhaps my devotion will be an offering to the future. And so, I spend my time looking and looking.

* * *

The oldest of these images is a photo of Gerda Taro. There is a good chance it was taken on a small hand-held Leica. Maybe even her own camera. Maybe by the Canadian who was with her when a tank careened into her. The black and white is genuine, not a filter like the one I use on my phone to make mundane pictures appear older and more artistic. The absence of colour is a form of time warp. The monochrome adds glamour despite the composition—the scene could be a still from a film set. Taro is in the foreground. Her eyes are closed, and her forehead is smooth. This feels notable, her smooth forehead, because she has been grievously injured and would have been in incredible pain. Her forehead is smoothed of pain's contortions. She is ethereal despite the blood coming from her nose and mouth. The blood almost looks like it could be stage makeup, except her stillness is unsettling even on film. The eeriness of her arrested movement soaks through the static image. She has the kind of hands that could model for diamond rings or dish soap, and here they are clasped and still. Even though her lips are closed, and though I couldn't say how, it seems that in the image she's still breathing. I wouldn't say she looks peaceful, but she does look like she is thinking about some quieter place.

By the time she died, Taro had been at least three different people. The name her parents gave her was Gerta Pohorylle, and she carried it from Stuttgart to Leipzig. She wore that name as she fled to Paris and her parents left Germany for Palestine. She never saw them again. After arriving in Paris, Gerta met Endre Friedmann, a Hungarian Jew on the same flight from anti-Semitism. He had a camera and taught her how to use it. Together, they experimented with how to catch an image to convey truth and render it visual.

Photography bought Gerta time, a little cash, and the right papers—French residency was being granted for journalists and taking photos got her half the qualifications she needed. There were still problems, though. Gerta and Endre took good photos, but their citizenship papers were wrong and so were their names—too obviously Jewish. So Gerta made a plan. They would build a fabulation, a photographer with a name to hail the right associations, the right affiliations, the right country. A name too slippery to be linked to wrong nations. Robert Capa was their invention. They would say Capa took all the photos. They'd pretend Endre was an assistant to Capa, because it was still a man's world, and through Endre they would sell their photos to the French photo agency Alliance-Photo.

It didn't work, or at least not the way they'd first imagined. Their editor recognized Endre and offered less money for their photos than they were worth because of Endre's Jewishness. Endre quickly came to understand he would have more success with a new name, one that pulled from the glitziness of Hollywood. Gerta knew this too, and so Endre took off his name and stepped into their invention. He became Robert Capa. It was one of those times in history when people could change names the way others might change outfits. Gerta changed her name too, building a stylish portmanteau to carry herself forward. From Greta Garbo's beguiling charm and the avant-garde imagery of artist Tarō Okamoto, she emerged as Gerda Taro.

Capa and Taro. These new names became passports, a way for the pair to move as borders were being shut. A way to circulate images that told the stories of what was happening to people on the ground. Their photos started to sell. Capa and Taro were pulled to more tumultuous locations. They circulated on their daring, wit, skill, and the glossy elegance of the

Golden Age of film. Their youth and beauty opened doors; their cameras became tools for truth telling. They held these cameras up to catch images of women shooting alongside men on the front lines of the Spanish Civil War, and children who had been killed by bombs while waiting for food. They got close to the violence so the world could see. Their adage: If the photos aren't good enough, you aren't close enough.

Capa got close, but Taro got closer. She was seriously injured by a tank while taking photos on the Brunete front. "Crushed" is what the headlines of the international newspapers read, but she didn't die on the battlefield. Instead, she was transported to a hospital and cared for by doctors, though they failed to save her from her injuries. The papers didn't publish the photo I have. Instead, the papers ran a photo of Taro smiling with Capa, or one of her with the troops, or her with the milicianas with their rifles, or her with children in a breadline, fists raised in the air. Taro's beauty—fine bones, wide eyes, and her narrow eyebrows arching toward the sky—seemed to promise something.

Her death caused a sensation: "First female war correspondent to be killed in action" reads one caption. Beauty and disbelief sometimes make headlines, so there she was in the papers, smiling, fist raised in solidarity or eyebrow pressed against the camera's viewfinder as she sought the right shot. She was twenty-six when she died.

In the photo on my computer, Taro is in the foreground, prone. Behind her, a Hungarian doctor named Janos Kiszely attends to her. Kiszely's body is bent toward Taro's in the shape of a C, bent in extreme care. His right hand is curled against his knee, a ballast while he crouches. Taro might be on the floor of the hospital; it is the only angle that makes his body make sense. He holds gauze against the corner of her mouth. His elbows angle wide away from her face. Careful, I imagine, not to touch in ways that hurt. Around the arc of his hand, I can see her eyebrows. They are thin and arched, the eyebrows of another era. How, on the front lines of the fight, did Taro keep her eyebrows so neat? I love her for it. In fact, it is thanks to her neat eyebrows that we know it is her in the photograph. Kiszely's son posted the photo on social media some time ago, and Taro's brows helped identify her. The photo had been in Kiszely's son's possession for years, given to him by his father's friend at a funeral. Kiszely didn't talk much about the war, and so his son had tucked the photo away without looking closely at it or the inscription on the back. Some stories require the dead to come back and tell them.

The inscription on the back of the photo, the one Kiszely's son didn't read, is partly wrong. It says *Brunete Front, June 1937 (in Torrelodones) Mrs Frank Capa = of Ce Soire of Paris, killed at Brunete*. The name is a mistake. It is possible the place and date are also incorrect. Though partners in photography, and widely purported to be lovers, Taro and Capa never married. The *Mrs* is a marker of the times. It's strange enough she was a woman at the front. To be unmarried was, it seems, a bridge too far. The other little oddity is the error in the name: *Frank Capa*. An amalgamation, maybe, of Capa and the famous Italian film director Frank Capra. What I like about this mistake is that Frank Capra too was a technology maverick. He recognized the possibilities of sound and made films with dialogue when wealthier, more established directors were slow to start producing "talkies." Also, Capra too got a foothold in his field thanks to a little fib about his experience in film (he had none at the time). Telling, maybe, of what it takes to get a good idea noticed.

I can relay the context, the details of this photo of Janos Kiszely wiping blood from Gerda Taro's face as she dies. Muse on the aesthetics and the politics. I can think *beautiful* and *horrible* and not be undone. Possibly, I am even inspired by the youth, commitment, bravery, and skills of these two people who travelled to fight a war that wasn't theirs. I don't know what compels me to return to this photo. To have copied it. To have moved it to my desktop. To return to it over and again without feeling bored or dulled or numbed. The problem is that this capacity—to look, to understand the story being told, and to have that story stick with me—retreats when I look elsewhere.

* * *

The scroll, I know, is a serious problem. I have looked at photographs documenting the death toll of imperialism and its ilk for as long as I can remember. When I was small, I could only get to the television room, deep in our basement, by moving through the room that held my father's collection of photographs of Civil War generals whose eyes followed me as I scurried, sock-footed, to the light switch on the opposite wall. I've been to battlefields and memorials where the documentation of names goes on for city blocks. I feel as though I have been trained to pay attention to history. "We go out of history, into history and the awful responsibility of time," my father would intone, paraphrasing. The quote was from the American writer

Robert Penn Warren, and the lesson was clear: pay attention, these things need witness. This is our ordinary job, mundane in its dailiness, holy in its purpose.

So why do I falter in my attention when I look at photos on social media? I cannot bring myself to witness, for sustained periods of time, mothers carrying bundles in Sudan, fathers holding bundles in Gaza, teenagers blown up in Ukraine. I cannot even look at a floundering polar bear or singed koala. There is something wrong with me, I tell a friend. The friend just nods and says she knows and feels it too. But what specifically is the problem? Is it because there are so many of these photos, the disasters they depict so disparate? Maybe it's a question of how they are presented to me on my phone's screen.

Or it might be a question of proximity. In *Camera Lucida*, the prolific Roland Barthes suggests that looking is work the viewer can undertake not just once but many times. "Confronted with the photograph," he writes, "it is the same effort, the same Sisyphean labor; to reascend, straining toward the essence, to climb back down without having seen it, and to begin all over again." Struggle, belief, readjustment. A commitment to the belief that the photograph and what it documents matters. That is work a viewer can shoulder. Barthes wrote *Camera Lucida* as he was looking through photos of his mother, trying to find the essence of her in images after she died. But the constant stream of photos on my social media feed of people in crisis seems, somehow, distant, no matter how urgent the situations depicted in the photos also feel. I cannot reach the close proximity that Barthes had with photos of his mother.

Of course, the work of looking at a photograph is also an encounter with technology. Whatever frames the photo—

whatever is literally outside it—structures our encounter with the image. Who took the photo, the circumstances that bring us to view it, and the shimmers of myriad other stories the image itself offers. All these are available to the viewer to consider. The skirt at the edge of a picture that indicates a person is just beyond the frame. An empty cup across from the subject of a photo. These are small and significant reminders that there is so much a photo can capture. And then there are the feelings a photo can evoke: the importance of a viewer's encounter with the photo and the feelings it conjures have the potential to change opinion, to shift our structures of feeling. The vitality of such an encounter flaps its wings on the periphery of my thinking.

* * *

When I look at the photo of Taro, the force of my feelings arranges itself neatly, with conviction. But when I look at other photos, photos in an endless catalogue of accumulation, I lose myself, and time, to the scroll. Sometimes, I am moved to hot, unstoppable tears that lead to weeping that shakes my whole body. Other times, I am a cool observer, wondering if I have lost any sense of goodness. When I resurface from the endless scrolling, the endless accumulative potential of the infinite now, I feel actual shifts in my neural pathways happening, and this frightens me. Most of the time, the photos collage themselves together, collapsing individual stories into one long wail. Sometimes, the photos flick in front of my mind's eye unbidden after I put my phone down, a mark of what I have witnessed from the quiet of my kitchen.

One photograph that plays itself on repeat in my mind I first saw on Instagram, captioned only as "A father in Palestine." I can see it behind the closed lids of my eyes. The man is bent at the hips, and he is holding a small bundle in his lap. His pants are soft brown, and his shirt is pale yellow. The bundle he holds, tenderly, is white. This man in the photograph reminds me of Kiszely, bent with the care of not wanting to cause harm. But this bundle is a child, clearly dead. Its face is still and round as a moon. I saw this photo for the first time on Father's Day. I thought of my own child's father, rushing down a hospital corridor the night she was born to follow the nurse into a testing room. There is no good sentence I can fashion to describe this photo, surely. My words fall short, and yet I am compelled to try again.

I turn off my phone. And still, my body shudders. I turn the phone back on, press a few buttons, and take a screenshot. I send the photo to myself and open it on my desktop, beside the one of Taro, eight decades and countless caring hands between them. And beyond the frame, all the technologies and stories before this moment, held still on film. What is all my looking for? Is the photo "Father in Palestine" good enough—is it close enough, in the way that Taro meant?

I didn't ask these questions in the first moment of looking because my words were thin in my mouth. Instead, my body shuddered with the wordless labour of distant witness and I wondered whether that witness would ever be enough.

Shuddering is the body doing work. My therapist explains this when I tell her about how, after a shock, my body trembles beyond my control. Try as I might, I cannot stop it. Of the shudder, trauma theorist Cathy Caruth suggests there is a kind of catharsis that can occur through it, but I am not sure this applies in this context. I think of Italian philosopher Giorgio Agamben who, in his meditative book on witnessing and the shame of survival, thought the watcher might take on what words can't carry and hold what they've witnessed instead in their own body. He names this carrying the "flush of shame." This is what one feels when witnessing the degradation of another. The shudder, yes, the camera shutter.

I need to look and look well; take in an image and not be adrift in the scroll. "Adrift in the scroll" is my phrase for what philosopher Mark Kingwell names the brand of boredom that dominates us because of our immersion in technologies of distraction. The phone promises both distraction and connection, but it delivers consistently only one of them. When I look at the photos on my desktop, isolated from anything but each other, I feel something different. I feel the shudder.

The third photo I keep returning to is of my daughter. One focus of my partner's scholarly work is on Canadian involvement in the Spanish Civil War. This means we often have a reason to travel to Barcelona, and it has become one of our favourite cities. In the photo, our daughter is standing in Barcelona's Plaça de Sant Felip Neri. On the second-last day of January, in 1938, an air raid by Franco's fascists dropped bombs on this square that housed, and still does, an elementary school. Forty-two people were killed, most of them children. The attack on Plaça de Sant Felip Neri was the second-deadliest bombing in Barcelona during the Civil War. The school walls are still riddled with pockmarks.

Plaça de Sant Felip Neri is small and unassuming, easy to miss if you aren't looking closely. In the photo, you can tell the day is hot from the small damp marks on my daughter's shirt. She stands with her back to the camera. She is wearing black stretchy pants that show her ankles, and a grey-and-black polka-dotted T-shirt that she has improbably tucked in. She has her hands flat against the hollows in the wall, and on her left wrist you can see a plastic beaded friendship bracelet. The smallest sliver of her face is visible beyond the curtain of her hair. Only cheek and eyelashes, enough to tell she is looking at the wall in front of her, getting as close as she can, working something out. What you can't see is that just before the photo was taken, my partner knelt down beside our daughter and explained to her what had happened in this square. He spoke quietly. I couldn't hear what he said above the noise of school children in the courtyard. When they finished talking, our child stood up, looked at the school kids, and put her hands on the scarred wall.

* * *

"All portrait photography is fundamentally performative," writes feminist performance studies scholar Peggy Phelan. What she means is that the framing of the subject by the photographer is built around desire and lack. We look for the subject in the photo, but what we find is both them and not them. We get what Jacques Lacan refers to as the *lure*. I go to an image with a desire, with want, and what I receive is not the meeting of my deepest desires but something else. A pose, a moment frozen and disaggregated from the mess of life. When photos are stacked, one atop the other, in a social media feed, I suspect the lure works differently. The organization and encounter of image after image with no frame or context changes both attention and desire. My attempt to look, to pay attention. Yoked to the deeply ingrained impulse to consume and accumulate, I consume social media feeds with no pause, no intention.

The three photos on my computer screen are not really portraiture. There is no way—save for the one I took—to tell if they are staged or planned. Even the suggestion feels like violence, at least in the cases of Taro and the grieving father. As for my daughter, staging her (if such a thing were possible) would also be a form of manipulation. Instead, I think now that these photos are about proximity and the work of looking.

If the photos aren't good enough, you aren't close enough. That's what Capa and Taro believed. Perhaps one of their most famous collaborative photos is of a young Republican the instant he is felled by a fascist bullet. *The Falling Soldier* documents the moment the young fighter is killed. We see him, head back, arms wide, his right hand still wrapped around his rifle. The photograph made Capa's reputation and has been haunting him ever since. Was it staged? The speculation was immediate. I'm not so sure I mind if it was. Capa and Taro were artists bent on witnessing destruction. They wanted to document the raw physics of truth, like how and where bodies fell. They also used photos to highlight urgent truths about real people being killed. When I look at *The Falling Soldier*, or Taro's photos of women lying next to one another shortly after they were murdered in a German air raid, I am moved and enraged. Taro's photo of a group of tenement farmers, fists raised in the No pasarán salute, makes my pulse quicken. I am looking at these photos to find courage to act, because courage is there over and over and over again, looking back.

Closeness—the feeling of proximity—has changed in my lifetime. In this moment in history, there is a shift in how the closeness of looking happens. I scroll past images on my phone—a school being disinterred, an advertisement for wrinkle cream, a father sitting in a pile of rubble holding his dead daughter's hand after a catastrophic earthquake. Another school shooting in America. Another missing woman whose absence is signified by a red dress hanging in a tree. Another trans person murdered for the outrageous act of wanting to live. And the police, always the police. The genocides that don't get photos. The ones that do. The ambient and constant violence of racism that punches holes in the everyday, every day. Eventually, I always look away, ashamed and bothered.

It is a predicament, isn't it, the desire to be connected to the world, and yet to also be so overwhelmed by its images that a kind of boredom comes creeping in? The algorithm, which I have perpetually participated in and shaped, is also shaping me. Between images of beautifully made linen clothing are pictures of the dead, dying, and disenfranchised, of a million injustices. I know all this, yet seeing it still shocks me—these jump scares of the cascading scroll. I can move through them slowly, or I can move through them quickly, and there is always more. The five-hundred-dollar handmade silk dress. A mother holding her own precious bundle, bereft. An ad that offers good things for my sweet dog's gut health. Students being tear-gassed. Colleagues and friends demanding the government recognize that art = work. The massive volume of photos, the accumulation of the banal and the horrific, sap the images of their power. It is impossible to look fully, to truly take it all in with care.

Even the smallest survey of twentieth-century reflections on the photographic encounter reveals tension. Agamben writes of the difficulty of reading absences in the archive of genocides. Those absences, he emphasizes, are not random, but the banal evil of bureaucracy. Choices get made; someone decides what is worth including in the historical record and what is not. There is nothing quite as boring, or, in certain circumstances, insidious, as bureaucracy. Franz Kafka knew this too, and in his novel *The Trial* he shows the reader that modern bureaucracy is an evil that is absolute. Consider too Hannah Arendt, who wrote a tome on the origins of totalitarianism that can be glossed by one of her phrases: "the banality of evil." Being bored or dulled by detail is a dangerous tool that too many already know how to employ. Cultural theorist and critic Sianne Ngai names this kind of state of shock and boredom and overwhelm *stuplimity* and suggests it is a key aesthetic of this century and the last. I don't want the photographic encounter to be a kind of slow violence that keeps company with banality and bureaucracy, with the distance that stuplimity fosters. Beyond the dissociation that repetition—grid after grid of human-made horrors—there must be the punctum of the image. The thing that gets me nose to nose with what is lost without forgetting how it was lost in the first place.

Between the immediacy of the image and me looking at it, a set of feelings happen. It's not exactly that I'm bored; it's that the edges feel both sharp and beyond my grasp. Of my feelings on the photo of Taro's deathbed, I wonder: is the difference in the delivery? The constant presence of colliding images is not new. A newspaper would fall with a thump on the doorstep in 1936, and you'd bring the images inside your home. You can't scroll past a material object. You have to pick up the paper with its headlines and its disasters and choose: read or discard.

If the photo isn't good enough, you aren't close enough. But these three photos on my desktop are both good enough and close enough. It is me, the looker, the one who must calibrate my proximity to what each photo captures. I think of a story I was told about the first time Picasso's *Guernica* was displayed in Spain, shortly after Franco's death. The massive painting is meant to be seen in a relatively small space so that the viewer can't avoid the horror of the massacre. A few weeks after it opened at the Reina Sofia, gallerists couldn't figure out why there was a strange shadow on the opposite wall. Then they realized: it was scuffing from people backing up to try and take the whole painting into view. Their blue jeans left the marks on the wall, traces of attempts to calibrate witnessing. Whether that story is true or apocryphal is the work of the now.

There is a new responsibility to look closely. To learn what it means to witness, and to apprehend the responsibility that witnessing creates. That is the urgency my three photos triangulate. The urgency to look carefully and with intent. The urgency to give attention and time. The urgency to calibrate our proximity to others. We need witnesses with their camera phones rolling, recording all the violences, yes. And we need witnesses to sit with images and give them the dignity of time.

Something shifts again when I give my time and attention. I get closer. I gather the arched eyebrow of a dying Gerda Taro. I gather the father, his bundle, all the bundles I have scrolled past and past and past. I gather my child, hands against a pitted wall where she is looking hard to understand. I gather them closely in my mind's eye, these photos and their stories, side by side, at all hours of the day or night. During all the waking hours, which know no usual clock, I turn back to these photos and look and look and look.

ON ENCOUNTERING AGNES MARTIN

I believe in living above the line. Above the line is happiness and love, you know. Below the line is all sadness and destruction and unhappiness. And I don't go down below the line for anything.

Agnes Martin

What I knew about Anges Martin could fit on the head of a pin. It wasn't until a writer I love mentioned Martin that I found myself scrolling pages and pages of her work. I was looking for an image to serve as the cover of a book I was editing of this friend's work. Their writing—vital, exacting, thrilling—stalks issues of gender and culture with the movements of a wolf. The book needed an image that was contradictory without being hypocritical, one that was filled with strange beauty. It needed something that conveyed tension without falling into despair. If this writer thought Agnes Martin was *it*, then I wanted to know everything.

Martin's work felt to me like interior landscapes and ecosystems. Memory, place, and feeling rendered in colours, shades, and lines. Canvases awash in monochromes, lines that walked between delicate and sharp, and grids and grids and grids. Computer screens are poor windows through which to peer at objects made by hands, but needs must. I landed on one of Martin's works from the 1990s called *Happy Holiday* and expanded it until it filled my whole screen. The work, mainly acrylic paint and graphite, is, in real life, five feet by five feet. The colours are, to my inexpert eye, first a pink that hovers between salmon and a species of rose called Elizabeth that gives off incredible perfume, resists saltwater's corrosive powers, and lives in my mother-in-law's garden facing the Atlantic. At the same time, the pink is the colour of the bottom of a young cat's paw. The painting's second colour is an off-white the shade of a gallery wall that has become muddied and chafed by people walking by it for years on end. Leaning backs, brushing elbows, thoughtful backsides have all given the off-white a patina of weary, decadent filth. It is a shade that has seen some things.

I loved *Happy Holiday* and wanted it for the cover of this writer's book. The image was, in the end, far too expensive for a small press's permissions budget, and we settled for an excellent photo the writer had taken. I mourned the Martin, though. *Happy Holiday* seemed to hold contradictions in its colours and lines. It was not *un*happy, but it felt as though any happiness it contained had come at a cost. It reminded me of horizons, of hope, and of some other feeling that is a mix of having come through darkness and a chipper kind of resolve. I am more aware of my resolve than I was in my younger years, and if pressed, I could point to a timeline and say *there*, that is the place where my resolve wavered in the face of what was needed. Put your finger on the spring of 2020 and press down. There. That is where I wavered. That is one of the places I slipped below the line.

Before 2020, the word *pivot* had some shimmer to it. You might pivot sharply away on your heel, a swift and meaningful departure from some untoward turn in conversation. Or you could watch a mobile of birds and clouds pivot lazily on its axis above a child's bed as their small chest rises and falls. But when the world held its collective breath in March of that year, the exhale that followed forever changed the word. To *pivot* meant to make it up from scratch again, no sense of whether *it* was working. For me, a teacher, *it* meant trying to convince students of the music and magic of language when they were sinking below the surfaces of their suddenly shuttered lives. Class after class, students disabled their video, and more of the little squares on my computer screen went black. No words, not even faces. *Pivot* was a word so overused it began to lose its shape and bag at the knees. Everything was pivot. We were living pivot lives. All turn, all reinvention, no time to stop and feel the effects of the turning on our bodies and our minds. A teacher friend once had all their students hold their laptops up to the sky as each class ended. My friend would take a screenshot and send it to the students, those little grids of blue and grey meant to remind them that despite it all, they were there, together. Same sky, each day. Same sky.

In the earliest days of the lockdowns, my daughter and I would leave the house and walk to the Halifax Common. A large stretch of green in the summer and white in the winter, the Commons is usually filled with ballplayers and cricketers and folks who suntan nearly nude as soon as the mercury hits ten degrees Celsius. Usually there are dog walkers and skateboarders and children climbing in the one low tree that seems to bend itself precisely to that purpose. That spring, there was no one. The government had closed parks and beaches and marked acceptable walking routes with tiny orange flags. The Commons' huge green space was a grid of little orange lines, and one step off could mean a fine that cost more than our rent. And so we walked, my child and I, in the orange corridors, trying to make a game of it. "How many flags can you hop past on one leg? Let's try counting in twos. Run as far as the seventeenth flag and then come back to me." My attempts at whimsy were puny. My mind felt more flag than line, fluttering in the wind while my child, then four, smiled gamely. "Okay, Mama," and she was off and back again so quickly I had to take to wearing sunglasses despite the clouds, for that spring I could not stop crying. Her willingness to reach toward lightness; my incapacity to swim back from the feeling of sinking further and further down. Lines of flags on the grass, lines of wetness down my face, the lines my child ran between me and the next tree.

* * *

Agnes Martin was born in Macklin, Saskatchewan, a border town known for its annual bunnock festival. Bunnock, or bone throwing, is a game involving lining up a row of bones, moving back several paces, and tossing more bones to knock the standing ones down. On one hand, bunnock is a version of any number of set-'em-up-knock-'em-down games. On the other, the macabre elements of bunnock feel significant. Thought to have been created in Siberia to stave off boredom and despair, the game was imported to the prairies by Russian immigrants. These were former Minister of the Interior Clifford Sifton's ideal immigrants, the ones he wrote about in the early 1920s as vital for settling the Canadian west. These immigrants had focus, grit, and little else, according to Sifton. They could survive the hard cold, the stark landscape, and the demands of starting over in a strange place.

Martin didn't stay in Macklin, though I wonder if throwing bones would have appealed to her, what with the game's order: the straight lines of the bones standing up, the white arc of a bone through air. She moved to America before she was twenty and became immersed in New York's art scene. She lived in a loft, made friends and lovers and art, and though she did accept medical intervention, on the whole Martin managed her schizophrenia, which for her included auditory hallucinations, on her own. Management meant developing ingenious sets of routines and rituals. It meant exhausting her body and mind with those routines and rituals in order to bring quiet. It meant painting lines and grids over and over. Set up those bones, knock 'em down, do it again. Stave off the despair.

* * *

So we had our routes. To the Commons and across its pathways, past the empty skate park and the climbing tree. "Hello, tree," my daughter would call, and that would be enough to undo me. I started to suspect there was again something seriously wrong with me. Steady on, keep an eye on the path and where to go next. We'd pass the high school, with its empty windows, and continue down to the horse stables, a remnant of the previous century in the centre of the city. The horses were out in the paddock most days that spring, as if they knew we needed them to carry emotional loads rather than bodies on their backs. We began to recognize other walkers who came to see the horses daily, as we did. That was the spring of knowing glances and chin nods. No words needed; no extra exhalation wanted.

Sometimes you could see a horse's name engraved on a small metal disk on its halter. A large palomino named Sadie took a liking to my girl. To be immediately loved by an animal is rare magic. Blocks before arriving at the stable, we would begin to look for Sadie, though we couldn't possibly see the corral quite yet. "Will she be out? Will she remember me?" My daughter would pick flowers for Sadie, bring her stuffed animals to show her. And, whenever we rounded the corner and Sadie was there: elation.

Each time my heart was in my mouth, each time I was set to yell, *Watch out! Be careful! You are so small. The horse is so big! Your body, her hooves.* Each time I bit my words and watched as my girl would talk to this soft-eyed animal, unpack her little bunny-covered backpack for show and tell. Then it was time to trot together. Can you imagine? It seems impossible to me still. My girl would run, and Sadie would run with her. Back and forth, up one side of the corral then back, only a tiny fence made of posts and plastic between them.

I seemed to be on pivot, too. I stalked the inside of our home like a large mammal in a small cage. I fingerpainted and papier mâchéd in a fury, made more furious still because I did not know where the rage was coming from. Then my girl would turn her sweet round face toward me and ask for more. More crafts, more reading, more make-believe, more undivided attention from my deeply divided and distracted mind. In theory I wanted to give all this. This—the giving of time and attention—was part of why my partner and I had decided to invite a child into our house. And yet. How many times did I walk down the hall to hide my face in another room? That's a statistic I do not care for. I was below the line of happiness by leagues.

Buddhist Chögyam Trungpa writes that to be fully present, we need to allow ourselves to be tender and sad. To feel it all, in other words. I have moved through periods of my life when the bell jar of depression has dropped. Other times, the opposite happens: I feel nothing. This period—of pandemic, of pivot, of early parenting—was something different altogether. In hindsight, it feels as close to an embodiment of acute bother as I can conjure at a cellular level, though I didn't recognize it as such at the time. Nothing was clear save for the sharpness of my emotions and a deep sense that things were beyond my control, because they were. My hypervigilance—over germs, my feelings, the feelings of my most loved ones—didn't matter. Indeed, it was possible I was making things worse. I didn't want to over-focus, and yet it also felt distinctly like I was missing important moments. Things were getting lost as time became spongy.

While I was underwater, my partner took a different path and started making plans. As soon as the borders unlocked, we'd leave. We had some time owed to us by our employers and we would take it. This leaving was another line of logic

I couldn't imagine, but nonetheless I opened my palm to his world-making magical thinking. *Pull me up*, I would have said had I been able to put words to what I was feeling. In 2022, when the Covid-19 pandemic was still very present, my family and I went away for a full year. As soon as we were allowed to see people again, we left for places where we knew no one.

Before our departure, I took our child's pointer finger and placed it on a map of the world. "We are here," I said. "We will go here." I traced a line with her finger from our small port city across the blue of the Atlantic, through Europe and its web of borders, across the Middle East, through Southeast Asia, pausing briefly on the punctuation of Japan, then floating her finger over the Pacific and the expanse of North America. We land, with an exclamation, back where we began. Leaving was a strange choice, maybe, so quickly after years of isolation, bubbles, and pivots. We were desperate to test the lines between home and everywhere else. And then there was the window of the world the pandemic shut. "We went into this young," my partner said, "but we've come out of it middle aged." It was true, and that felt like another line, only this one crossed off what came before and counted down days toward what was yet to come.

That is how we found ourselves, some months and a million miles later, standing in the Artist Rooms of the Tate Modern in London after an ordinary, if less than magical, morning. I'd woken, groggy and irritated, to the grey walls of a too-costly, rundown hotel. The rain outside looked cold and heavy. It was impossibly early. Most mornings in our family, the edges are smooth. The whole organism and each of its discrete parts are working well. The thing—the choices you've made individually and together—runs like a dream. But some mornings it is not like that at all. This state of affairs is manageable, except on those rare days when it is not. Not fine. Not ordinary. Not even recognizable. There is life—your good life—with its inevitable bumps and crags, and on those rare mornings there is also the ghost of all the paths untaken. A panoply of ways you're failing, large and small. Or perhaps that's just me and I'm saying the quiet part out loud: that no matter my exterior, on the interior there is sometimes a wildly anxious and unconsolable creature.

There we were, amid the hush and swish of people looking at art. It was one of those hard-edged mornings, for me, at least. And me, I was agitated. Unsatisfied. Irritable and close to tears. I stood back and watched my daughter. She was seven. We were far away from the ritual of our horses, of the structure of seeing the friends who were back in school. Though, I realized standing in the Tate, that even before we'd left, we'd been seeing the horses less. Sadie had died from complications of colic. Gone were the days when our daughter and her friends communicated by leaving chalk messages in front of each other's houses and playing catch on FaceTime. "Are you seeing this?" I'd texted my friend, the other mother, as our ingenious and exuberant children invented ways to play together apart. "Yes," she replied, as they joyfully caught and threw their balls in separate houses, together. "Yes," I said too, but I didn't say "and I am crying," even though I was. I didn't miss the intensity of those times, yet I knew the feelings of panic could return at the drop of a hat or a frown appearing on a small face.

I thought all this as I stood in the gallery in London, watching my child take in the art, feeling my ugly feelings with their hard-to-name referents. I was exhausted by everything, most especially my own inability to put my finger on one singular thing and name it. This. *This* is what is wrong. That's what I wanted and couldn't achieve. No matter the amount of rigour or grace I offered myself, I couldn't name what *this* was.

* * *

Agnes Martin left New York for Taos, New Mexico, after the artists' co-operative she'd lived in was slated for demolition. In New York, she'd had friends, lovers, and comrades who supported her art. Taos was different. It was open space and relative solitude. In New Mexico, Martin spent years building a dwelling by hand. She used natural materials—mud, straw, wood—and constructed the structures herself. Only after her living and studio spaces were finished did she return to painting. The grids returned, drawn with mathematical precision. Her lines were measured and rendered by hand. Martin painted and painted. She believed that daily life, its practices, rituals, and ordinary moments, were superimposed over a kind of sublime natural perfection. Her mind still needed tending, and so she tended, with vigilance and structure and ritual. Layers of paint and lines over the beautiful, unknowable world.

Martin did not start writing until later in her career. So much of her written work is about managing emotions. Her self-discipline, her management of her own chronic illness, can be discerned in her writing. There's her reflection on lines—above is happiness, and below is sadness—which she sees as a horizontal *x*-axis. Incredibly, Martin claims not to go below the line for anything. What does Martin mean by "happiness" or even "sadness," really? She doesn't mean some sort of coercive script or intelligible narrative that makes her life make sense to others. Rather, happiness and sadness are portmanteaus. Crack them open and worlds of nuance spill onto the floor. Happiness and sadness for Martin seem to be shorthand for benchmarks against which to gauge herself honestly. Happiness and sadness are lines marked on a wall. Our feelings and our passions are something else altogether. There are, for Martin, passions that move through us. These are what she calls "the exhaustibles"; they pass quickly. Their opposites are the inexhaustible passions. The inexhaustibles are "within the mind," writes Martin, and they "go on forever." A *y*-axis coordinates with the *x*-axis of happiness. Together they make Martin's plane upon which she plotted points against their origin. I think of this as the abyss.

* * *

I've left us in the Artist Rooms on a rainy, irritable morning in London. We were in the city as a treat to ourselves. There we were, on sabbatical; it was what we'd dreamed of, saved for, worked toward for years. I carried small and big struggles in my body like luggage I was reluctant to put down. I pulled them to the forefront of my memory and rolled them around often. These struggles proved something to me, but what, I still couldn't say. What was clear was that anything less than a wonderful time at the gallery felt like failure to me. Terminal exceptionalism, I could name it now, or a kind of narcissism bathed in benevolence. We had to live above the line! If we didn't, I felt, surely this was not just a failure but a harbinger of additional failures to come. Intimate failures. Failures of the self. Of me.

In the rear-view of my memory, it is difficult to conjure just how sharp and close to the surface these feelings were. How difficult they must have been to live with, for myself and my best loved ones. But as we navigated an exhausted child who did not want to marvel at modern art so much as she would prefer to watch a program on a device, I was well below the line. Our feelings were barometric, and the pressure was palpable. In that moment I needed to pull myself up and out of this place, and, in an attempt to do so, I took a photo of my daughter.

She was standing with her back to me, her hair in a messy French braid, the hairbrush having become a mortal enemy. She was wearing her constant grey hoodie, but in this moment the hood was down. Perhaps that's what caught my eye. Or maybe it was the stillness of her focus. She had her head bent low and was writing in her notebook. It took a moment for me to realize she was standing in front of a painting by Agnes Martin. She was writing with purpose, in front of alternating lines of white and washed-out pink. She held her pencil with the careful concentration of a surgeon. Her bottom lip just inside her mouth, folded in absorption. Her whole body bent toward the notebook, then curved up to the painting. Notebook. Painting. Notebook. Painting. Lines on the page, lines on the wall. I held my phone up and took a photo. Click.

Later, I asked what she had written. She held her notebook up to me with two hands. *Happy Holidays by Agnes Martin* it read in her carefully formed penciled letters. She must have noticed the card on the wall beside the painting and copied it. Beside the phrase there are three check marks. I ask what they are for. "For the three of us," she says, as if it were obvious, drawing a line under the checks with her finger.

* * *

"You're the only one that can discover for you the meaning of anything," Martin said once in an interview. "I don't mean intellectual meaning. I mean, what it means, how it makes you feel. You have to see whether you are really happy or not. Whether you are really sad or not. And you have to investigate what goes through your mind." This exploration, a kind of plumb line of the soul, reminds me of a collaboration between the founder of psychoanalysis, Sigmund Freud, and his grandchild. The collaboration is more well known as Freud making observations on desire and repetition by watching his grandchild process absence. Fort/da, or here/not here, became central to Freud's thinking on our senses of self and safety in *Beyond the Pleasure Principle*. The scene was this: Freud watched his eighteen-month-old grandchild drop a spool of thread over the side of the crib. When Freud's daughter Anna brought it back, the baby did it again. Over and over. Gone, and back again. Here, and not here. What I like is that regardless of the child's imperatives or whims, his actions made his grandfather think of what is there, and what is not. How things go far until they might come back again. The line between hope and despair is a taut strand of cotton thread thrown over the side of a crib and reeled back in.

Happy Holiday was painted in 1999. Martin drew from specific good memories to conjure perfection on the canvas. Perfection was a ruse, of course. She wrote that all her work "is about perfection as we are aware of it in our minds" but cautioned that the paintings "are very far from being perfect—completely removed in fact—even as we ourselves are." Each of her paintings from this period have titles pulled from Martin's memory. *With My Back to the World*, 1997. *I Love the Whole World*, 1997. *Faraway Love*, 1999. The titles of her work plot a course from the interior to the exterior. The line leading from our interior hearts to the things and people we love is imperfect, perhaps, but the procedure is luminous. We get to see the artist trying to move herself elsewhere through the labour of making art. Her living and working became ritual and meditation, yes, but also a manual for her survival. The patina of the off-white is not a single colour, but what comes from painting over layers of other small points and lines. This is a lesson I have learned from Martin: to do the work is to do both the labour and the art itself. Her living became a practice of living above the line, no matter what. The painting is the proof of that work.

In her extraordinary engagement with her own depression and the work of Agnes Martin, poet Victoria Chang also thinks about lines. As she tries to name and wrangle her own sadness, Chang turns to Martin's lines for company. "Agnes tells us to hold our minds empty and tranquil as they are, and recognize our feelings at the same time," she writes, before admitting that she wants to ask Martin how to do both at once. In my own attempt to do both, I imagine gossamer threads of spider silk tossed to the people and places of the past. I imagine pulling the threads, the joy of retrieval. Here you are, and there you go. I imagine how all of this requires a resolve that is washed-out pink and worn-out white.

A line in the sand is not the same as a line on a canvas. The line in the sand is a moment in time that, when crossed, changes things irreversibly. For a bit, I thought the line in the sand was March 2020. That the line in the sand might appear in two lines on a nasal swab test, or the lines marking out the metres we were supposed to keep between one another in the grocery store. I've drawn lines to other moments, marked them as transformative. They might be, but what I've gathered from Agnes Martin and three check marks drawn by a seven-year-old's hand is this: the axis I carry inside myself is the one that needs plotting first.

ON LEAVING THE HOUSE

Let's imagine how unspoken scripts can become a kind of inertia. Houses you are meant to want. Marriages too. Trajectories you take to tick the right boxes. Plot lines that make you intelligible to others. Now let's ask a question: What does it take to knock a girl off her frenetic forward track? What interrupts the conventional narratives that worm their way into the unconscious, the ones that whisper "you should?" What is enough force, figuratively speaking, to nudge a girl through the door?

Twenty years ago, the girl put on a black-and-white strapless dress, shoes she'd bought to cheer herself up after her dog had been hit by a car, and she walked down a hill to get married. She was twenty-five. The future was a flat, bright line, bigger than a prairie sky, thrumming with static. When she was a child, that same hill had been good for picking wild strawberries and the little purple flowers her grandmother called Johnny Jump-Ups. She walked down the hill dutifully. There is no other word for it. It was a bright day, but not sunny. In a picture someone took of the girl, the colour is blown out, but I can see that she is also carrying a wool shawl. Later, in other wedding photos, the shawl is wound tightly around her shoulders and she stares to the left of the camera. Her face looks like one in a daguerreotype, there but not, eyes always following movement, never quite still. She looks as if she has retreated to a room in her mind. Perhaps she is building an exit. Perhaps she is thinking her shoes are a bit too big.

* * *

The marriage shoes were so flat they could have been lines on a highway. They reminded me of pen-and-ink drawings in a couturier's notebook. They came to a point at the toe, which was engulfed by a huge brooch covered in fake rubies. The shoes were lined in hot pink, and a sketch of a cat in the style of French cartoonists took up much of the footbed. The shoes, of course, were mine. The girl was me. I find it easier to hold myself at a distance, as if I were an unknown character, in order to puzzle out my own strange actions. What I was thinking, as I stared over my cousin the photographer's shoulder, was this: the shoes were utterly unlike anything I had ever owned, and I loved them. I had worn them to walk away from a city I loved and back to my parents' home with a man I did not love but did not know how to leave. Would these shoes now walk me to a different, better life? Never mind that better was a white rabbit in a snowstorm.

The truth is, I have left many places and many people. Once, I ejected myself from a small cabin at the bottom of a western mountain. I drove my 1989 Oldsmobile Cutlass Ciera across the country and right into the middle of Montreal. It was 2002 and I had just lived out a year in a ski town known for avalanches and alcohol poisoning. Neither a skier nor a binge drinker, I'd spent the year learning how to bank the fire in the cabin's kitchen and helping the town's senior citizens log onto the internet at the library. I showered at the town pool and saved all my change to buy coffee at the café. My roommates were in the midst of a glacially slow breakup, and so keeping the literal home fire burning was my job. I'd just moved back to Canada from the southern United States and had precisely zero skills in the banking of fires. I could, however, order food in Italian, write a decent sestina, and identify the difference between Tuvan and Inuit throat music. University was finished for me, the planes had flown into the towers, and I had effectively relocated to the moon while all my American friends were planning protests. That year in the mountain shack felt like a fever dream. By the time I got to rue Sainte-Catherine in Montreal, the anti-war protests were becoming anti-globalization protests. I had missed a lifetime and lived two.

Montreal became my city. I didn't speak the language, though I tried. I had no people there; I arrived knowing no one and lucked into a sublet through the older and cooler daughter of my mother's friend. I arrived with my car and a fellow who helped me make the drive. I got rid of the fellow and kept the car. I enrolled in graduate school and immediately bought a leather hat that made me feel and look like Charlie Chaplin as the Little Tramp. I walked endlessly, at every hour of day or night, relishing the city's restlessness. I met people. I made friends. I became familiar with the barometric pressures of the place. I struggled through classes and started inhaling critical theory and cigarettes. I carried books by theorists like Jacques

Derrida and Julia Kristeva around in my second-hand blazer pockets and got into arguments about how best to represent class consciousness aesthetically in a text. And then I met a person who, for better or worse, stuck around a little longer than the car and the cat.

* * *

The trouble with fragmented stories is seeing how the pieces fit together. The other trouble is something I have come to think of as the void. It's everywhere, this void. It can spread, multiply, descend, or leap when I least expect it. It doesn't belong to me alone, and I have learned its different names. Evagrius the Solitary (345–399 AD) named it the Demon of Noontide and said it pounced most readily between the hours of two p.m. and ten p.m. Some call the void hell, and they say it keeps no polite hours. A careless girl could fall into it at any time, and then what? No coming out the other side like Alice, with a new bunny friend and a pocket full of magic stories. It seems to me that whatever its name, the void is both a mist and a pit. Atmosphere weaponized, but against what? The connective tissue called progress? Perhaps. The idea that a girl could make a whimsical house of her own mind and be happy there with an animal companion? Again—perhaps. In any case, it appeared to me the only way to outwit the void was vigilance and speed. Run forward as fast as you can. But what if, in the end, you run but don't get anywhere?

I gleaned early and young that love and sacrifice were the same thing. To care well for another meant to walk along the edge of the void. When I was in grade school, I spent a summer learning these lessons at a church camp run out of a basement in small-town northern Ontario. What I remember of that church basement was that it was cold, even on a summer day. Crepe paper decorations hung to brighten things up. A bulletin board was decorated with art by the congregation's children: Easter eggs and crosses, a cave with a black hole that should be a stone, rolled away. Everything made with construction paper and crayon, but still the room was blunted of colour and had the feel of a twelve-step meeting place. A piano sat in one corner. In another corner stood an easel with a large pad of paper, and the easel could be pulled in front of a small circle of chairs whenever someone needed to illustrate a point or make a list. Sometimes, if the speaker needed both hands, the easel was used to hold props.

The camp teacher was a woman I liked a lot. When she wasn't running camp, she worked in the local department store, which was a cross between a Sears, a Dollarama, and a hardware store. Men's pyjamas, a socket set, and fireworks were stocked in the same aisle. It was a place of pure possibility. I loved that store, even though it had a vaguely chemical smell that made me feel nauseous. One day in particular, she brought to camp a series of laminated pictures, including one of a farm. This was new. I crossed and uncrossed my ankles with excitement. The story she then told us was about a mother hen and how much she loved her chicks. The mother hen was a separate image that could be Velcroed to the farm scene. She was also laminated, and she had soft white feathers glued on her back and wings. I wanted to touch them to my cheek, so I sat on my hands. Good children do not fidget in church.

The story went like this: the chicks were mischievous, and the mother hen busied herself with teaching them where to peck for the best corn, where to get fresh water, and to wait one's turn. The teacher drew these small details out for us. I felt mischief in me, a chick as well. I wanted the warmth of the mother hen and her steady discipline. But then the story took a turn: one night there was a disaster. The henhouse caught fire, never mind how, and there was no way out for the mother or her babies. I listened to the camp teacher, stunned. In the morning, when the farmer discovered the ruins, he came upon the mother hen's body, charred and still smoldering. Here, the teacher pulled off the laminated mother hen's lovely white feathers and exchanged them for a black heap of crumpled paper. I thought of heaven, and how surely this was where their story ended, mother and babies ascending into light. I was only half wrong. The teacher told us that just as the farmer was about to carry the mother's body away, he heard a sound. Tiny, weak, and coming—could it be?—from beneath the mother's body. The teacher plucked the crumpled black paper off the mother and pushed the hen into her skirt pocket. As she did so, she turned her back for a moment, and then she returned to us with a flourish. In her hand were several small yellow pom-poms. "The chicks!" she declared. "Saved by their mother's brave sacrifice."

At the end of the lesson, each child was given one of the yellow pom-pom chicks to keep. I held mine in my small sweaty palm as I walked upstairs into the sunlight. I did not want this lesson, which was that a mother should stay in her house when it is burning to shelter everyone with her body. I did not want the mother's body to be a dead metaphor for martyrdom, where her only choice was to freeze her own desire and offer others shelter. I did not want metaphor at all. I did not want the familiar arc, and yet it worked on my small mind, told me what exactly it was women were for. What it was to mother well.

* * *

I have left many people and many places, but others I eye with a hunger for what I think they might feed me. What can Marguerite Duras mean when she says that in a house "one can be so alone as to lose one's bearings"? What about the home of one's own habitual thoughts? When is a void a hole, and when is it a portal? When should a girl run away from the danger, and when should she run toward it?

* * *

In *As I Lay Dying*, William Faulkner's famous novel of fragments, the youngest child imagines his dead mother as a fish. This is the only way he can metabolize the impossible image of her coffin slipping into the river water as the family tries to find a way to cross. Can I borrow from this book to explain to myself how, in the twenty-first century, a girl got married and moved into a home against her will? Or rather, against her better judgement. *Will* might imply rational desire, according to Thomas Aquinas. He thought that humans couldn't move toward that which does not appear to them in the moment to be good.

There was little that could be called rational in what I did in the decade of the wedding shoes. I'd started well. Survived a small town, carved space for myself in a big university, kept it weird, smoked cigarettes, drank whiskey sours, and danced. Made the dean's list. Dabbled in food service and almost got a real job at a publishing house. But never, ever, did it seem to me that I was in charge. I wrote my own story, but I also had expectations that weren't mine written onto my unconscious. If the mind is a house, mine was in disarray, pulled in too many directions yet still firmly on track. The track was an intelligible life.

My feet, which are small and square, never fit neatly into my pointy wedding shoes. They buckled the leather at awkward places, marring the long lines of the shoe's design, but I did not care. The shoes had been purchased in a boutique in Montreal some months before the wedding for more money than I could afford, but what did it matter? The morning I bought them, my beloved dog had gone out for a walk with the neighbour and was returned to my doorstep dead. She was a hound dog from the prairies of southern Alberta, a dog used to stretches of land filled with possibility, and I had brought her to heel in Montreal, right in the centre of that city. I was bereft for weeks after she died. I walked the park close to my house where she and I had just begun to meet other dog walkers. I practised explaining her absence in my scratched-record textbook French. "Mon chien? Elle est morte. Renversée par une voiture. J'ai du mal à respire en pensant à elle. Comment s'est passée ta journée?" But no one asked after her. I was slick with sorrow. It wafted off me.

Home was impossible without her. The little rooms of the ground-floor apartment that I'd painted so carefully were revealed to be in fact garish and unbearable. My hands were loose and felt ridiculous as I moved through the city without a lead in them. I was haunted by the sense I kept forgetting something vital, like my pants or my passport. She had been so pretty, this dog, that shopkeepers would invite her in while I browsed books or tested the skin of a peach. "Mignonne!" they would coo. "La plus chouette!" And now, there was just me, unremarkable except for the dog-sized hole in my heart that I tried to fill with wine and coffee and walking and impractical, expensive shoes. The dog had been some sort of compass, an indication that the path was good and therefore I was too. She would look at me with her big cow eyes and know without being told when it was time to get up and walk out the door. It had been new to me, this shared sense of the weather. With her in my life, something in me woke and lifted its snout to test the wind's direction. It strained at its lead, that internal creature, and pulled in different directions I didn't yet have words to name. There was nothing to do but lilt along with the stronger creature beside me. No need for intelligibility with her by my side. Once she was gone, it was me who came to heel beside the script of an intelligible life. Surely marriage was what came next, right?

* * *

Okay, so, look: Elena Ferrante has a word for this fragmentation. These jumps. *Frantumaglia*, she calls it. The jumble of fragments. A storehouse of time without the orderliness of a story. Perhaps the jumble is my order, the fragments of a story put together in the rear-view.

* * *

Twenty years is either a lot of time or none at all, depending on your metrics. So is ten minutes. And what if the real stake is not my memory but a portal that can open when the functional distance between things is removed? What if the habits of thinking, my bewilderment with that younger self, my bother at the elliptical and recurrent flight path of my hardest moods, is a symptom of larger system failures? After all, it is a wise girl who always knows the weather. I used to think of that girl who did not run, who instead tied up her hair and her heart and who dutifully walked down the hill, as evidence of some sort of poor design in my bedrock. A fault line. But I am beginning to look at her in another light. There are so many ways to survive in harsh environments. Sometimes the surviving happens before one has the language to describe the survival.

Walter Benjamin noticed a jarring calculus in his thinking about the changes modernism was bringing to the ways people saw themselves in relation to others. He used the language of architecture to think about the separation of public and private space. Benjamin described this bleeding together of separate states as "the substitution of the void for the home." But if the home is both inside the self and also the barn that can be burned down by others, there must, surely, be more outcomes that are possible. If I don't want duty, and I don't want to die in a fire just to be told I am intelligible and good, surely there must be another path.

But wait. I've made a fundamental oversight. When Duras talks about getting lost in the house alone, she's talking about the solitude of writing. I found this essay in Duras's collection called *Me & Other Writing*. At the end of her life, she published this series of essays on her craft and how she'd honed it. The house built by a writing life shelters her with a different kind of solitude, one in which disorientation better allows her to see her state clearly. Duras says, "it is in a house that one is alone. Not outside it, but inside. Outside, in the garden, there are birds and cats... One isn't alone in the garden. But inside the house, one is so alone that one can lose one's bearings." And so, when Duras outlines her house and the solitude it affords, she's talking in two directions at once. It occurs to me that in the house of thinking and writing, what you lose is the referent for the self. That referent for the self is outside the house—it is society. What you lose in Benjamin's modern swap of a house for a void is your bearings without the social sphere and its stories of progression, but it is necessary to lose your bearings for a while in order to write the interior life. Because a house of writing is also the deep interiority in which the portal can open and take Duras somewhere far from where she is; where I might be.

I come back to Duras for her willingness to rest in ambiguity. This woman knows that not everything wraps its arms around language in a welcoming embrace. Some states are hard-edged, and others are white-hot. Somehow, Duras's writing builds a shelter that houses those feelings. "She made a language...: that cut as close to human subjectivity as it is possible to get without dying of pain," writes Deborah Levy in an article celebrating Duras's writing that walks so close to the void. Perhaps some of us are like my long-gone dog from the prairies, running hard, eyes focused on the horizon's hot line.

Of course, I didn't stay in the marriage house, though its hard edges were made softer by adopting a new black dog who never left my side. This house was another track from which to derail. What's more, the walls of my real, unwanted house came crashing down. I mean this literally: One morning I walked out the door, and when I returned the walls were piled on tables and counters, covering the couch, turning the new dog's black fur white with their dust. There was nothing intelligible in those stacks of broken walls, and so we left, this younger dog and I. Rather, the dog and I left the loneliness of the real house and the stifling air of an outwardly intelligible life. We loped out the door together, not easily, but easy in each other's company, and left the uncanny home for the garden path, and did not, like Lot's wife, look back.

ALL THE WAKING HOURS

If you are here, you know by now that the bankers are useless, though dangerous; kings are flies; the craven philosophers, with some of their poet friends, have left for the mountains; and the rest of us, we are somewhat bored with it—all of it—and somewhat overcome.

Canisia Lubrin

On the wall across from my desk is a framed self-portrait by the artist Sarah Lucas. Lucas sits in a wooden armchair. Her legs are relaxed, but her hands grip the armrests. She is wearing torn jeans that look effortlessly cool, and her grey T-shirt is tucked in. She looks directly at the camera, unsmiling. On each breast there is a single fried egg. Sunny side up. There is a package of cigarettes by her right foot, and an ashtray. These objects suggest she's been there a while, but her posture says otherwise. I like everything about this image, especially her expression. It is often described by critics as defiant, but I see something else. I see the don't-look-at-me-that-way that has morphed into caught-you-looking-asshole. I see the steel that comes with endurance and the humour required for living under ruinous conditions that we're told to think of as normal. I see an artist who has turned her tits into breakfast and in doing so made meaning out of the mundane.

On the corner of the same block as my office, in 1971, John Baldessari contracted students from the Nova Scotia College of Art and Design to act as his amanuenses. For an exhibit in the mezzanine space of the Anna Leonowens Gallery, Baldessari paid students to produce work on his behalf, instructing them to write the sentence "I will not make any more boring art" over and over until the walls of the gallery were covered from floor to ceiling. It was a bit of a sensation then, and it would grow in notoriety throughout the years. The piece has been read as Baldessari's critique of elitism in his artistic context. Some critics understand it as a kind of scolding of his contemporaries. However, Baldessari's letter to the gallery director explaining the project offers something of a different view. It opens, "life is hard... life is earnest." The letter goes on to explain Baldessari's commitment to an art practice as a means of addressing these truths—that life is hard and earnest—head on. It turns out that in addition to his attempt to make art more engaging, Baldessari was also trying to reprimand himself. It was he who was trying not to make any more boring art. The thing is, writing the same phrase over and over is boring. So, too, is watching a documentary about not making boring art. At least, this is what our ten-year-old told my partner when they went to view a recent installation at the wonderful Art Gallery of Nova Scotia.

"Bored with it—all of it—and somewhat overcome," writes Canisia Lubrin in *Code Noir,* a collection of short stories that infiltrate a set of violently oppressive and racist laws written by King Louis XIV. That's where the rest of us are left, now that the poets and the craven philosophers have headed for the hills. Bored and bothered. That's the thesis of my thinking—now hunt for the question. Search for the part of the question that sticks with you, makes you sit up straight and cock your ear to listen. Sniff out the keywords; be a good forager. Root out the feelings that structure your days, find them, truffle-like, in the dirt of your own thinking.

* * *

Toward the end of Robert Penn Warren's 1946 novel *All the King's Men*, Jack Burden, the beaten-down witness of the story's unfurling, has a realization. He thinks that history and time are an "awful responsibility." It is a weighty place to land, but then the book, which is set in the American South, is built on weighty ruminations. Not quite the lugubrious poetics of William Faulkner, it is nonetheless a novel concerned with the ebb and flow of time as it works on human responsibility and whether it is possible to act in an ethical fashion. It is one of those books that feels epic in its scope. It also feels American. That used to mean modern. Now, I think, it means something else, though that's a line of thinking for another time.

Jack Burden is a political reporter who, despite his misgivings, is swept up in documenting the meteoric rise of Willie Stark. Stark is everything career politicians seem to lack, at least initially. He is grassroots. He is a man of the people.

He accomplishes significant gains for his constituents. And, of course, he is flawed in banal ways. He treats women like shit, and eventually he extends this abuse to everyone close to him. People are shattered and come back for more. They say "thank you" while thinking "never again." Stark tastes power, likes it, and lets it ruin him. The novel is, in fact, a repetition of abusive acts. He is caught in a feedback loop of history: try as he might, Stark can't break out of the cycles of power that reward him when he walks all over those he is meant to protect and serve. Jack Burden is aware that he's not much better than Stark, yet there he is, bearing witness to the carnage. It is dismaying to read *All the King's Men*, in part because the failures of these characters are so familiar.

I first read this book over a series of afternoons and evenings when I was twelve. This is—in retrospect—a ludicrous time to be reading such a book, but it was my father's favourite, and I was moderately precocious when it came to reading. I was also extremely bored. We had recently moved from Ottawa to rural North Carolina, from the suburbs to the middle of nowhere. I was shy, and my father had a huge collection of books. After I worked my way through the leather-bound editions of the Everyman's Library Classics, after I finished *Wuthering Heights*, and after I finished all the George Eliot and Thomas Hardy I could get my hands on, I looked up. It made sense, in a way, that my father gave me *All the King's Men*—we had just moved to the shimmering heat of the American South. I was learning lessons over long, boredom-drenched afternoons, but I didn't yet realize it. Those lessons, I see now, had something to do with time and attention; with boredom, bother, and the land that stretches between those two points.

We left the winters we knew behind us, but I learned we didn't really leave much behind, for mine are a nostalgic people. Time, it was conferred upon me, was a thing heavy with responsibility. Time was also protestant, by which I mean not to be wasted. Idle hands are the devil's playthings, after all. It was difficult to hold these lessons alongside the ones I knew in my body: time stretches across days, weeks, and years at different speeds. It sometimes becomes familiar in its shapes and moods. Afternoons spread out dreamily each summer. Sunday evenings are moody. Some weeks, the bell jar of sadness dropped. Internal tensions emerged about what to do in, and with, time. Familiar cycles darkened the windowsills of my mind like Poe's raven harbinger. When I thought of it, I turned to literature to help me make a story out of these tensions, though sometimes I was so taut I forgot to look for help. I forgot to think of anything at all.

* * *

Jack Burden is a figure on whom the responsibilities of time rest heavily. I found another in the work of Marguerite Yourcenar, who defied easy categorization in her life as well as her writing. Her collection *Coup de Grace* contains a short section that completely distorts the reader's relationship with time, gender, and the shape capitalism makes of our lives. It was published in 1939, and I encountered it in a university classroom seventy years later, sometime in the early spring when I found myself in an increasingly familiar place of sadness and self-loathing. These states—call them what you like—have been with me periodically for most of my life. Sometimes they arrive with some predictability, and other times they appear with the rapidity of a light switching off. I am most lonely in these times, and unlikely to seek company. Yet the strange figures that appear in Yourcenar's tale struck me as familiars sidling up, unbidden and ready to work their strange magics.

Yourcenar's story opens with hollow-eyed creatures standing, transfixed, before a messianic image. It takes a moment to realize they are on a city sidewalk. A twenty-first century reader might misrecognize these figures as detainees in a death camp or residents of a city under ceaseless bombardment, but we would be wrong. Yourcenar's figures are children. They are standing on the sidewalk by their mothers, who have been rendered motionless before a shop window. On the other side of the large pane of glass is a display of cleaning supplies and organizational solutions. These women stand inert, made zombie to their desires, for an incomprehensible amount of time. The children—there appear to be legions of them—become less and less human as the wait goes on. Time is a durational practice shaped by the desires of these women, who in turn have had their desires shaped by the constraints and expectations of their social world. They are transfixed, but unsatisfied. As amanuensis of the interior Lisa Robertson writes, in our current long cultural moment "we cannot fix our object. We are anxious and bored and must shop. With this scribbled grooming we hatch ourselves anew." Wanting and waiting. Women tied to what they are told to want, and children shaped by that wanting too. Yourcenar's story ends there. No resolution. No hope. No apologies. Here we are, Yourcenar seems to suggest, tied to time and our desires. Bored to death, anxious, unwilling or unable to move our little feet or tug at the arm of our companion. As I read this story in one of my sad springs, a little seed was planted. I discovered, in retrospect, that what I was coming to think of as boredom had valences.

I have found these subjects—boredom, bother—interesting in part because they re-entered my days palpably when I became a mother. And while these actual things filled my days, their attendant worries and ruminations began to inhabit my nights. This time, though, they entered with the added complexity of having to keep a small child alive. In a rush of hormones and sleeplessness, of overwhelm in the form of love and shock, all the waking hours and their affects took on sharper relief. Time reorganized itself. Boredom and bother expanded and contracted. Anxiety furled outwards while I worked keenly to keep my outsides looking calm. I began to think swirlingly in the expanse of an early spring when freezing rain gathered on the ground.

1:00 a.m. I reflect on leaving the city after a hard winter.

1:30 a.m. I am shaken, shaking.

2:00 a.m. I am used to filling every minute of my time with action and calling that meaningful, calling myself useful.

2:30 a.m. This is a learned behaviour, and it makes me efficient in my own way.

3:00 a.m. I was, for a few decades, used to having command of my own time, and then that changed.

3:30 a.m. I think of how boredom gets mixed up with sadness. I think of years of hustling on the edge of precarity and suspect this has led me to a place of endless restlessness. I think of my diagnosis of clinical depression at the age of seventeen, of the pills that followed, though there was no other follow-up. I try to recall something of that time that might be helpful now.

I remember a psychiatrist who came from the city to the country once a month. I remember being pulled from class to visit her. I remember after the first visit driving myself to appointments in that Oldsmobile Cutlass Ciera, the one I bought with my own money. I remember the psychiatrist sending me to the closest city, a big one, with a university hospital. Blood tests and questions: a lump in my throat as I try to answer them. My reluctance to take the prescribed pills. My mother and aunt taking me for lunch. Why was my aunt there? No matter.

4:00 a.m. Depression might be a public feeling, yes. A feeling that others suggest reveals something of the current moment. I think about Ann Cvetkovich, who writes about depression as an archive. Where do I house my own personal records of despair?

4:30 a.m. I think of Sylvia Plath's brilliance. About the incandescent experience of reading *The Bell Jar* for the first time and feeling not horror but recognition. How good it feels to be seen by a book, or by other readers. In third-year university, some girls from poetry class invited me to join their Tragic Poetess Softball League. We sat in the shade, smoked, read poetry, and talked about the violences our bodies knew.

5:00 a.m. How familiar the descent of the bell jar feels when it comes with its accompanying darkness. How familiar and how banal.

5:30 a.m. Why is middle age the place where so many of my favourite writers came to die?

* * *

For much of my life, the bell jar has temporarily descended. When lowered, it mutes colour, and makes soft things hard and quiet things loud. This is both figurative and literal. I was thirteen the first time it happened. I felt as though my brain was an Etch A Sketch, and what was erased was any sense of purpose or meaning. I was diluted of interest, either distanced or feeling everything too much. The next time the bell jar lowered, I was older, better at smoothing my public self while my private one curled into a ball of self-loathing. Each time it lifts, this glass jar that stands in for an emotional state, the distance I have travelled in my mind is more familiar.

Now the bell jar descends less. Not never, but far less. Feelings now have horizons to them and no longer seem like they will stretch on forever. It can get almost—yes—boring, this sense that I have a steady frequency and a steady place in the world. But even monotony can be monstrous in its own way.

Take Virginia Woolf's story "The Mark on the Wall," which starts in medias res. The speaker can see from her desk something that was not there before, a mark. Her wonder at what made the mark leads her down multiple tributaries. She makes associations, leads the reader's attention elsewhere, then reminds herself of her task. Each time an associative fancy is aborted, she brings her attention—and the reader's—back to the mark. Something is on the wall marring its blank expanse. Or perhaps *mar* is the wrong word because sometimes the mark becomes an organizing principle. A place to rest both thoughts and eyes. "There's no harm in putting a stop to one's disagreeable thoughts by looking at a mark on the wall," the writer reflects. From this frame of mind, the mark becomes "a plank in the sea" clung to by an exhausted swimmer. It is "something definite," "something real," "full of peaceful thoughts." Like some cognitive behavioral therapy trick, the mark on the wall is a place to rest a busy mind, to connect it to the body. No longer an intrusion or a sign of poor housekeeping, the mark offers stillness and transcendence. It reminds the writer that she has these capacities and wells within her. And then, just as she's reached this place of realization, everything shifts. She is interrupted by a presence in the room. Someone stands over her and says they are going out to buy a newspaper, though "it's no good buying newspapers... Nothing ever happens. Curse this war; God damn this war!"

What a juxtaposition: "nothing ever happens" and the "war." This mash-up of nothingness and catastrophe is both boring—the shared state that makes nothing happen—and it is the void into which millions of lives are sucked. In the same breath that war is rendered both boring and banally evil, the newspaper buyer pulls the veil from another mystery. "All the same," they say, "I don't see why we should have a snail on the wall." The essay ends with the writer's realization: "Ah, the mark on the wall! It was a snail." The divine Anne Carson observes of this abrupt ending that what's surprising is not the snail, but that the reader grasps immediately that the person interrupting is a man. The mark on the wall, the place from where wild reflections spring, is stripped of its mystery. Story done, woman told.

Boredom and bother moved, for a moment, into something else. And then with a bit of dialogue, narrative time returned. It is not unlike my bell jar, which can bring a sudden smothering of capacity. And it shows just how quickly the unexpected can descend on any of us.

I thought about Virginia Woolf one morning, sitting in the sun at my kitchen table. I had just finished watching a video on my phone of a man speaking to a reporter about the relief he felt when, after two days of waiting, he was told his eight-year-old daughter had been found. Found dead, I should say. The camera pulls focus on the man's face as he explains that dead is better than every other scenario he had imagined in the hours while he waited for news. I sat in a sunbeam and wept. In the hole where his child was, I pictured the face of my own.

I have done this many times: visualized my most precious loved ones in spaces left by bombings, well-being check-ins, or simply wearing hoodies. This is my attempt to apprehend the loss of others, and my grief does double time as I picture both real and imagined atrocities. And then I am horrified anew at the speed with which I can encounter violence and return to my routine in my sunny kitchen. What does empathy accomplish when it can be turned on and off like a light, I wonder. The daily work of being both stimulated and dulled, made sharper by atrocity.

It reminds me, again, of Hannah Arendt's concept of the banality of evil, which carries at its heart an almost inconceivable contradiction: that people can do evil things without themselves *being* evil. That marinating in the bad acts of the world will sour some of us in the end. Ordinary evil is so matter of fact, so unremarkable, that it can be absorbed without someone noticing. We, all of us, are drenched in it. I sit with this phrase, "the banality of evil," as I scroll through feeds and encounter evils of all kinds, including my complicity in looking and then looking away. I have tried, from time to time, to immerse my attention fully in the evil in front of me, to witness, witness, witness. My attempts sometimes catalyze curiosity and other times despair, or worst of all, banality. Too often, I end up bored with all of it and somewhat overcome.

I've adapted that phrase—bored with it all, and somewhat overcome—from Lubrin's *Code Noir*. "If you are here," Lubrin begins, and I read "here" to mean another place, a place where we gather our disparate yet connected experiences. This is the state between boredom and bother. Not beyond, not outside, not disaffected, but between. A shared place where some of us find ourselves. Find each other, perhaps.

Spring is leonine where I live, the weather crisp and the days colder than they have any right to be. Another war has started. I've lost count of how many that is since our child was born. I've also lost count of the roar of more bureaucratic horrors, as the province where I live announces catastrophic cuts to funding in arts, culture, and other public sectors. No more bus passes for teenagers who need to take transit to get to school. Child-care centres have had their operating budgets slashed with no warning. Long-standing provincial funding for graduate students has been cancelled. Effective immediately, a bell jar has slammed down in its usual way.

All of this is sharp, and none of it is new, not really. Amid the sinking feeling of familiarity, the disappointment and boredom of recognition that yes, again, the playbook of those with power is so brutally predictable and banal, I walk with our child to the artist-run centre down the street. When we enter the building, we are welcomed by people who know us from time spent there over the years. We pull up chairs, fetch tea and snacks, and begin painting signs for a rally that will be held in a few days. My daughter makes a sign for her dad to carry that reads *No Art? No Heart*. We make extras to share. When we leave, we hug several people we know.

Once, when she was small, my daughter broke the silence of a nighttime car ride to crack her first joke, which was about the moon. Now, after sign-making, we walk home holding hands under that same moon. My waking hours—all of them—remain filled with hard truths and with my attempts to witness them. All the waking hours I get are also filled with softness and intention. I am here, paying attention and painting signs. Animated by my little red heart and my concern for others. In the house I've built with my partner and our child, there is a brown dog and a grey cat, several hundred records, and room to share supper with others.

"Boredom is the threshold of great deeds." Walter Benjamin made this big claim when he was writing about witnessing seismic shifts of urban development. Benjamin was trying to document a speed of change that was outside his control, but that was still affecting him in the most granular ways. Rather than rest in the uneasiness and alienation between so much and not enough, he made this claim, and then he followed it with a question: "What is the dialectical antithesis to boredom?" Maybe this question—or his ability to question, to remain curious—was Benjamin's great deed. I wonder. Perhaps the dialectical antithesis to the boredom created by dangerous bankers and buzzy kings is to understand myself in the "us" that is the rest of us. I concede that so much of this work—the acts of care and witness—is boring, but I also wager that no matter how we feel about it, the work remains. I will continue to scrape my nail against the hard feelings. To question. To witness. To keep the poets and the writers and the artists near, because their work widens the horizons of the possible. Their work, just past the threshold, where the great deeds of attention and care happen.

NOTES

On the Public Risks of Being Bored and Being a Woman

Winnicott, D. W. *Playing and Reality*. Tavistock Publications, 1971.

Cvetkovich, Ann. *Depression: A Public Feeling*. Duke University Press, 2012.

Cassian, John. *How to Focus: A Monastic Guide for an Age of Distraction*. Edited and translated by Jamie Kreiner. Princeton University Press, 2024.

Weil, Simone. *The Need for Roots: Prelude to a Declaration of Duties Toward Mankind*. Putnam's Sons, 1952.

Goyette, Sue. *The Brief Reincarnation of a Girl*. Gaspereau Press, 2015.

On Wisdom and the Weather

Robertson, Lisa. *Lisa Robertson's Magenta Soul Whip*. Coach House Books, 2009.

On Swimming

Duras, Marguerite. "Motherhood Makes You Obscene." *Me & Other Writings*. Translated by Olivia Baes and edited by Emma Ramadan. Dorothy, a publishing project, 2019.

Freud, Sigmund. "The Uncanny." *The Standard Edition of the Complete Psychological Works of Sigmund Freud, Volume XVII*. Translated by James Strachey. Vintage, 1999.

"Royal Commission." See Gislason, Donald E. *The Icelanders of Kinmount: An Experiment in Settlement*. ICCT, 1999.

Hoffmann, E. T. A. "The Sand-Man." *The Best Tales of Hoffmann*. Edited by E. F. Bleiler. Dover Publications, 1967.

Bataille, Georges. *The Tears of Eros*. Translated by Peter Connor. City Lights Books, 1989.

Dey, Claudia. *Heartbreaker*. Vintage, 2018.

"'Offensively tasteless' Mother Canada statue plan sparks outrage against PM." *The Guardian*. June 26, 2015.

Plath, Sylvia. "The blue hours." *Ariel: The Restored Edition*. Harper Collins, 2004.

Freud, Sigmund. "Concerning the factors of silence, solitude, and darkness..." ibid.

On Style as Survival

Warner, Sylvia Townsend. *Lolly Willowes; or, the Loving Huntsman*. Chatto & Windus, 1926.

McSweeney, Joyelle. "Style As Survival: On Writing After Death." *Literay Hub*. March 25, 2024.

Janis Joplin photograph from 1969. See "Remembering the life and career of Janis Joplin." *New York Daily News*. January 19, 2023.

Arendt, Hannah. *On the Origins of Totalitarianism*. Harcourt Brace, 1951.

Lorde, Audre. "The Master's Tools Will Never Dismantle the Master's House." *Sister Outsider: Essays and Speeches*. Crossing Press, 2007.

Billie Holiday photograph from 1949. See San Francisco Digital History Archive. https://www.foundsf.org/index.php?title=File:Billie-Holiday-at-the-Hall-of-Justice-on-a-narcotics-charge,-Jan.-22,-1949-BANC-PIC-130089.01.jpg

Acker, Kathy. *My Mother: Demonology, a novel*. Grove, 1994.

Nina Simone photograph from 1998 taken in the lobby of the Dorchester Hotel by Steven Double. See Rockarchive.com. https://www.rockarchive.com/prints/n/nina-simone-ns001stdo

On Collision and Witness

Lyotard, Jean-François. *The Postmodern Condition: A Report on Knowledge*. Translated by Geoffrey Bennington and Brian Massumi. Manchester University Press, 1984.

Levy, Deborah. *Swimming Home*. Bloomsbury, 2012.

MacDougall, Duncan, scientist of the twenty-one grams experiment. See "Hypothesis Concerning Soul Substance Together with Experimental Evidence of the Existence of Such Substance." *Journal of the American Society for Psychical Research*. 1.5 (April 1907): 237.

Twenty-one Grams. Directed by Alejandro González Iñárritu, 2003.

Betts, Doris. *Souls Raised from the Dead*. Knopf, 1994.

On Looking and Looking

Taro, Gerda. See ICP: International Centre of Photography, *Gerda Taro*. https://www.icp.org/browse/archive/constituents/gerda-taro. See also *The Mexican Suitcase*. Directed by Trisha Ziff, 2011.

Barthes, Roland. *Camera Lucida: Reflections on Photography*. Translated by Richard Howard. Hill and Wang, 1981.

Caruth, Cathy. *Unclaimed Experience: Trauma, Narrative, and History*. Johns Hopkins University Press, 1996.

Agamben, Giorgio. *Remnants of Auschwitz: The Witness and the Archive*. Translated by Daniel Heller-Roazen. Zone Books, 2002.

Kingwell, Mark. *Wish I Were Here: Boredom and the Interface*. McGill-Queen's University Press, 2019.

Phelan, Peggy. *Unmarked: The Politics of Performance*. Routledge, 1993.

Lacan, Jacques. *The Seminar of Jacques Lacan, Book IX: The Four Fundamental Concepts of Psychoanalysis*. Translated by Alan Sheridan. W. W. Norton & Company, 1977.

The Falling Soldier (full title *Loyalist Militiaman at the Moment of Death, Cerro Muriano, September 5, 1936*). See *The Mexican Suitcase*. See also "Death in Spain: The Civil War Has Taken 500,000 Lives in One Year." *Life*. July 12, 1937: 19.

Arendt, Hannah. *On the Origins of Totalitarianism*. Harcourt Brace, 1951.

Ngai, Sianne. *Ugly Feelings*. Harvard University Press, 2005.

On Encountering Agnes Martin

Martin, Agnes. *Agnes Martin: Writings*. Edited by Dieter Schwarz. Cantz Verlag, 1991.

Martin, Agnes. *Happy Holiday*. 1999. Acrylic and graphite on canvas, Tate Britain.

Sifton, Clifford. "The Immigrants Canada Wants." *Maclean's Magazine*. April 1, 1922. 16: 32–34.

Trungpa, Chögyam. *Meditation in Action*. Shambhala, 2000.

"You're the only one that can discover for you the meaning of anything," Martin said once in an interview. See Guggenheim holdings. https://www.guggenheim.org/wp-content/uploads/2016/11/guggenheim-agne-martin-speaks-about-emotion-and-art-audio-transcript.pdf#:~:text=I%20believe%20in%20living%20above,go%20down%20below%20the%20line

Freud, Sigmund. *Beyond the Pleasure Principle*. Edited by James Strachey. W. W. Norton & Company, 1961.

Martin wrote that all her work "is about perfection as we are aware of it in our minds." See *Agnes Martin: Writings*, edited by

Dieter Schwarz. Cantz Verlag, 1991.

Chang, Victoria. *With My Back to the World: Poems.* Farrar, Straus, & Giroux, 2024.

On Leaving the House

Evagrius the Solitary. *The Praktikos & Chapters on Prayer.* Translated by John Eudes Bamberger. Cistercian Publications, 1972.

Carroll, Lewis. *Alice's Adventures in Wonderland.* Edited by Mark Burstein. Princeton University Press, 2015.

Duras, Margurite. "The Sound and the Silence." *Me & Other Writings*. Translated by Olivia Baes and edited by Emma Ramadan. Dorothy, a publishing project, 2019.

Aquinas, Thomas. *Summa Theologica*. Translated by Fathers of the English Dominican Province. Benziger Brothers, 1911.

Ferrante, Elena. *Frantumaglia: A Writer's Journey*. Translated by Ann Goldstein. Europa Editions, 2016.

Benjamin, Walter. *The Arcades Project*. Translated by Howard Eiland and Kevin McLaughlin. Belknap Press of Harvard University Press, 1999.

Levy, Deborah. "All of Nothing: Deborah Levy on Marguerite Duras." *Literary Hub*. October 7, 2024.

All the Waking Hours

Lubrin, Canisia. *Code Noir*. McClelland & Stewart, 2023.

Lucas, Sarah. "Self Portrait with Fried Eggs." 1996. Digital print on paper, Tate Modern.

Baldessari, John. "I Will Not Make Any More Boring Art." 1971. Lithograph, Whitney Museum of American Art.

Baldessari's letter instructing installation. See John Baldessari holdings, NSCAD University. https://nscad.scholaris.ca/collections/0a8b847a-b589-4e0e-be13-914b5bf1b85e/search

Hubbard, Teresa and Alexander Birchler. *No More Boring Art*. Exhibition. Art Gallery of Nova Scotia Nov. 8, 2025 – Jan. 25, 2026.

Warren, Robert Penn. *All the King's Men*. Harcourt Brace, 1946.

Yourcenar, Marguerite. *Coup de Grace*. Translated by Grace Frick. Farrar, Straus, & Giroux, 1981.

Robertson, Lisa. *Occasional Works and Seven Walks from the Office for Soft Architecture*. Coach House Books, 2004.

Cvetkovich, Ann. *Depression: A Public Feeling*. Duke University Press, 2012.

Plath, Sylvia. *The Bell Jar*. Heinemann, 1963.

Woolf, Virginia. "The Mark on the Wall." *Monday or Tuesday*. Hogarth, 1921.

Carson, Anne. "Virginia Woolf and Thucydides on War." *Men in the Off Hours*. Knopf, 2001.

Benjamin, Walter. *The Arcades Project*. Translated by Howard Eiland and Kevin McLaughlin. Belknap Press of Harvard University Press, 1999.

ACKNOWLEDGEMENTS

Once, for a few weeks, I was a writer with other writers in a mountain town. We each had managed to carve twelve days from our regular lives to go live amidst rutting elk and grey mountain ranges. The aim was to write, and we were all enmeshed in projects that were called literary memoirs. What makes a literary memoir different from a non-literary one, I've decided, is its reliance on the figurative. Sometimes, metaphor can do more than facts and linearity to get to the heart of thinking. I was in awe of everyone in the group, including the mentors. I felt as though I had been admitted by clerical error. Yet, despite my deep imposter syndrome, I did not want to be sent home under any circumstances, and so I tucked my anxiety into my collarbone and waded into new circumstances. We were each given a room with a view as well as a writing studio. The luxury of these spare spaces remains incredible to me even now. In the morning, some of us would walk down to the glacial river and get in. For sixty frigid seconds, we sat in silence. Or not quite silence, for there was the sound of our deliberate breath starting fast then getting slower. The water moving past us made sounds too. The wind in the trees. My toes on the bottom, sliding into silt and growing numb. And then, the shift, from fighting cold to meeting it at its edge. We stayed a minute, and then some seconds more. There was no forward and no backward either. We were beside each other in an ice-cold river. It was enough. Thank you to Kyo Maclear, Elamin Abdelmahmoud, Jen Sookfong Lee, derek beaulieu, Joyce Chen, Rachel Mattlow, Jocelyn Parr, Ketty Nivyabandi, Raksha Vasudevan, Threya Almontaser, Soraya Roberts, Michelle Cho, Eden Robinson, Sadiqa de Meijer, Mattea Roach, Taslim Jaffer, and Hannah Griffin.

Thank you to writers and artists for making worlds and inviting people into them. Thank you to the independent booksellers and small publishers for making it all happen.

Thank you to Andrew Faulkner, Leigh Nash, and Debby de Groot for seeing what I was trying to get at. Thanks, especially, to Andrew for his care-full editing.

"On Swimming" was published in an earlier iteration in Stacey May Fowles and Jen Sookfong Lee's collection *Good Mom on Paper* (Book*hug, 2022). I'm grateful to them for their encouragement and support of the earliest parts of my thinking about how to embrace the feral strangeness of a mother's heart.

"On the Public Risks of Being Bored and Being a Woman" was published in an earlier form in *Brick, A Literary Journal*. I benefited more than I can say from the keen eye and deft skill of Allison LaSorda, whose editorial prowess made me trust her and want to be her friend.

I benefited from a Canada Council grant that helped get this collection going. Thank you to the Council and to my anonymous peers who saw something they deemed worth supporting in that early germ of an idea.

Thank you to the generosity of readers and co-conspirators who I also get the good fortune to call friends: Fazeela Jiwa, Sina Queyras, Julie Joosten, Geneviève Robichaud, Allison LaSorda, Sue Goyette, Hannah McGregor (a.k.a. auntie), Hannah Moscovitch, and Myra Bloom.

Thank you to the people who make up the rich tapestry of my every day, near and far: Katie, Tony, Louise, Hannah and Christian and Elijah, Nasha and Harriet and Charlotte and Rajni, Kate, Stephanie, Cooper, Simon, the winter potluck crew, all the Sackville pals, Asha, Fazeela, Ajay, Ayaan, Eric, Alysha, Freddie, Colleen, Jillian, Lily, Jade, Neta, Linda, Laura, Kit, the wonder'neath folks, colleagues who know who they are, my family both blood and chosen.

Bart Vautour, you are the best. Thank you for living this life with me, thank you for your belief in me. You make everything better, more delightful, and infinitely filled with curiosity. I'm so grateful. More, please.

E., you are also the best. Learning from and with you is the biggest gift we get to keep giving each other. How lucky are we?

PHOTO CREDIT: B. VAUTOUR AND E. VAUTOUR WUNKER

Erin Wunker teaches, researches, and writes in Mi'kma'ki where she is an Associate Professor in the Department of English at Dalhousie University. She is the author of *Notes from a Feminist Killjoy: Essays on Everyday Life* (Book*hug, 2016) and *The Routledge Introduction to 20th and 21st Century Canadian Poetry* (Routledge, 2022). She is also the co-editor of *Avant Desire: A Nicole Brossard Reader* (Coach House Books, 2020), with Sina Queyras and Geneviève Robichaud; *Public Poetics: Critical Issues in Contemporary Canadian Poetry and Poetics* (Wilfrid Laurier University Press, 2015), with Bart Vautour, Travis Mason, and Christl Verduyn; and *Refuse: CanLit in Ruins* (Book*hug, 2018), with Hannah McGregor and Julie Rak.

RECYCLED
Paper
FSC® C100212
FSC
www.fsc.org

Printed by Imprimerie Gauvin
Gatineau, Québec